Journey to the Cross
A Guide for Lent and Easter

Jim Branch

For Mom and Dad. Thank you so much for a lifetime of love and care.

Introduction

This book is an invitation. An invitation to join Jesus on his journey to the cross. An invitation to consider how we are currently living our lives and how that compares to the life that God desires to live in and through us. It is an invitation to fast and to pray and to give. It is an invitation to reflect and to repent and to deny ourselves. It is not a journey for the faint of heart, but is for those longing for more; a deeper and more vibrant relationship with the God who dreamt us into being. Therefore, it is also an invitation to joy and to life and to freedom.

This book is an offering of time and space, of prayers and scripture, of questions and reflections. My hope is that it might be a helpful companion for your journey through Lent and into Easter; the season where we celebrate the Paschal Mystery that death now always leads to new life. Therefore, although the journey we take together over these next days and weeks is a difficult one, it is also an incredibly hopeful one.

For this season is a time when we *set our faces to go to Jerusalem* with Jesus. It is a time when we see the enormous cost of our sin, as well as the enormous love of our Savior. It is a time when we celebrate the incredible mystery that life always follows death and that resurrection always comes after crucifixion. It is a time when we celebrate the truth that for God's people suffering and sadness and pain and brokenness and death do not have the final word, life—God—does. Thus, it is a season where we are invited to *come and die, that we may live*.

Lent is a forty-day period—not including Sundays— that begins on Ash Wednesday and ends on Easter

Sunday. It is meant to echo the forty days Jesus spent in the wilderness, as well as the forty days Moses spent on the mountain with God. Sundays are not included in the forty-day count because every Sunday is considered a joyful celebration of our Lord's resurrection — *a Little Easter*.

The word Lent is derived from the Old English *lencten*, which means "spring"; that transitional time between late winter and early summer in which our world begins to wake up from its slumber and come to life once again. Therefore, the season of Lent is meant to be a season of life and of joy and of hope. So come along as we journey with Jesus to the cross.

Ash Wednesday

Come to Stillness: Spend a few minutes in silence, allowing your heart, mind, and soul to come to stillness. This will make space within you so that you might be able to hear God's voice and receive his word.

Opening Prayer: Gracious God, today begins a beautiful season of reflection and self-examination. The days that are before me invite me inward to that silent, holy space where your Spirit dwells. This time and this season call me to see my life through the eyes of your Son Jesus, and to know the truth and the reality of your great affection. Give me the grace and the courage to enter the space that these days provide, with joyful anticipation of our union. May I open my soul to your presence and let your loving kindness flow over me and seep into the deepest places of my heart. I ask this for your love's sake. Amen.

Scripture: Joel 2:12-16

"Yet even now," declares the Lord,
   "return to me with all your heart,
with fasting, with weeping, and with mourning;
   and rend your hearts and not your garments."
Return to the Lord your God,
   for he is gracious and merciful,
slow to anger, and abounding in steadfast love;
   and he relents over disaster.
Who knows whether he will not turn and relent,
   and leave a blessing behind him,
a grain offering and a drink offering
   for the Lord your God?

Blow the trumpet in Zion;
    consecrate a fast;
call a solemn assembly;
    gather the people.
Consecrate the congregation;
    assemble the elders;
gather the children,
    even nursing infants.
Let the bridegroom leave his room,
    and the bride her chamber. (ESV)

Journal: What in this passage speaks to your heart these days? How?

Slow to anger and abounding in steadfast love.

I am always messing up and yet He still loves me.

How is the Lord asking you to "return to me" during this season?

by having me to multiple talks for Club in YL and pouring better at Running Shine groups asking deeper questions.

What does that look like?

I am reading my bible more and working more deeply into the different passages.

How is he asking you to *rend your heart*?

Stop having impure thoughts about wMrea and different fantasies. Stop lusting for worldly things like drugs or certain kinds of lifestyles.

Reflection:

The word *rend* (*qara`*) is used 64 times in the Old Testament. It means *to tear*, most often used in association with the tearing of one's garments in mourning, grief, or agony. In this particular instance Joel is calling us not to rend our garments, but instead to rend our hearts, which sounds incredibly painful. I mean, to be distraught enough to tear your garments in mourning and grief and agony is one thing, but to tear into your very heart is taking it to a whole other level. Why in the world would God ask us to do such a thing? Probably because <u>he knows the great healing and release and freedom</u> that will come about as a result of this rending.

"Tear your hearts open," he seems to be telling us, *"and allow your sins to come out, that the grace and love and cleansing of your God might seep in. You are carrying a tremendous burden. It has to be weighing so heavy on your heart and your life. Come to me. Return to me. Unburden yourself of the heavy load of sin. Give it all to me, for I will remove it as far as the east is from the west. Yes, grieve and mourn your sin, but, in the end, release it into my hands and walk away in the joy and freedom of having been forgiven. That's what this season is all about."*

Pray: Spend some time responding to God about whatever is going on in your heart, life, or world this day.

Closing Prayer: O Lord, thank you that you would rather I be torn to pieces than allow me to continue to be something less than I was created to be. Now that is true love! Help me, during this day and during this season, to return to you with all my heart. Whatever that may look like. Amen.

Thursday

Come to Stillness: Sit for a few minutes in silence, allowing all of the voices around you and within you to become silent. Then you will be able to hear the voice of your Heavenly Father when he whispers to your heart.

Opening Prayer: Lord I so want to make all of me ready and attentive and available to you. Please help me to clarify and purify my intentions. I have so many contradictory desires. I get preoccupied with things that don't really matter or last.

I know that if I give you my heart, whatever I do will follow my new heart. In all that I am today, all that I try to do, all my encounters, reflections, even the frustrations and failings and especially in this time of prayer, in all of this, may I place my life in your hands. Lord I am yours, make of me what you will. ~Ignatius of Loyola

Scripture: Matthew 6:1-18

"Beware of practicing your righteousness before other people in order to be seen by them, for then you will have no reward from your Father who is in heaven.

Thus, when you give to the needy, sound no trumpet before you, as the hypocrites do in the synagogues and in the streets, that they may be praised by others. Truly, I say to you, they have received their reward. But when you give to the needy, do not let your left hand know what your right hand is doing, so that your giving may be in secret. And your Father who sees in secret will reward you.

And when you pray, you must not be like the hypocrites. For they love to stand and pray in the synagogues and at the street corners, that they may be seen by others. Truly, I say to you, they have received their reward. But when you pray, go into your room and shut the door and pray to your Father who is in secret. And your Father who sees in secret will reward you.

And when you pray, do not heap up empty phrases as the Gentiles do, for they think that they will be heard for their many words. Do not be like them, for your Father knows what you need before you ask him. Pray then like this:

Our Father in heaven,
hallowed be your name.
Your kingdom come,
your will be done,
    on earth as it is in heaven.
Give us this day our daily bread,
    and forgive us our debts,
        as we also have forgiven our debtors.
And lead us not into temptation,
        but deliver us from evil.

For if you forgive others their trespasses, your heavenly Father will also forgive you, but if you do not forgive others their trespasses, neither will your Father forgive your trespasses.

And when you fast, do not look gloomy like the hypocrites, for they disfigure their faces that their fasting may be seen by others. Truly, I say to you, they have received their reward. But when you fast, anoint your head and wash your face, that your fasting may not be seen by others but by your Father who is in secret. And your Father who sees in secret will reward you." (ESV)

Journal: How will you order your Lenten journey? What will you include? What will you abstain from? How will you give? How will you pray? How will you fast? How are you intentionally going to make space for God during this season?

Reflection: There's a wise old saying that goes, "If you aim at nothing, you will hit it every time." This is particularly true in the life of faith. If we do not invest some time and energy considering how we might intentionally arrange our lives in a way that makes spiritual growth and transformation a possibility, it is unlikely that it will ever occur.

So, as we enter the season of Lent, it might serve us well to consider, at the beginning of this journey, how God would have us arrange our lives over these next days and weeks and months in order to make space within us, around us, and among us for him to move and to act.

Here in Matthew's gospel, Jesus offers us some helpful hints. He mentions three practices that might be of benefit in our Lenten journey. Three disciplines that might help us to make space for God to move and to act in our hearts, lives, and souls in the days and weeks ahead. The three things that Jesus mentions are: *when we give, when we pray,* and *when we fast.*

Giving, praying, and fasting have for centuries been a significant part of the life of faith as a whole. But particularly during the next few weeks of Lent a careful consideration of how these things specifically need to be a part of our rhythm and our practice could be to our advantage. For, as Richard Foster so wisely reminds us, *"If we want to live a life of union with God, it is not just going to fall on our heads. We are going to have to arrange our lives in certain ways."* Because if you aim at nothing, you will hit it every time.

Pray: Spend some time today simply responding to what God is doing within you; be it moving, or stirring, or drawing, or disturbing, or disrupting.

Closing Prayer: Help me, O God, to surrender my life completely to your control and command. Give it both a plan and a pattern that constantly reminds me of your presence and consistently makes me more responsive to your will. For the sake of your Son, Jesus, I pray. Amen.

Friday

Come to Stillness: Take a few minutes in silence to allow yourself to become fully present to God and to all that he has for you today.

Opening Prayer: Lord Jesus thank you for being willing to go all the way to the cross for me. Give me the strength and courage in the days and weeks ahead *to set my face* to go to the cross with you, whatever that may mean. In your name and by your grace I pray. Amen.

Scripture: Luke 9:51-55

When the days drew near for him to be taken up, he set his face to go to Jerusalem. And he sent messengers ahead of him, who went and entered a village of the Samaritans, to make preparations for him. But the people did not receive him, because his face was set toward Jerusalem. And when his disciples James and John saw it, they said, "Lord, do you want us to tell fire to come down from heaven and consume them?" But he turned and rebuked them. And they went on to another village. (ESV)

Journal: What do you think was going on in the mind and heart of Jesus as he *set his face to go to Jerusalem?*

What goes on within you as you hear these words?

What is your response to his willingness?

Where is God calling you to that same type of willingness?

What is your face set toward right now?

What would it mean for you to set your face to go to Jerusalem with Jesus?

Reflection: Jesus *set his face to go to Jerusalem.* And from that moment on the movement of his entire life and ministry would be toward the cross. It is a pivotal moment in the Gospel narrative.

The amazing thing was not *that* he set his face, but *what* he set his face toward. After all, each one of us *sets our face* on something, or someone—be it a job, or a skill, or a relationship, or a role, or an accomplishment, or a task, or a sport—but Jesus *set his face to go to Jerusalem.* He set his face not to achieve or acquire or accumulate, but to go and die. He set his face on obedience. He set his face on sacrifice. He set his face on love—and calls us to do the same, whatever that may look like.

So, as we journey to the cross with Christ this season, we are challenged to do the same. For we undertake this journey either as onlookers, or as companions. We can watch all that will happen over these next days and weeks from a safe distance—and remain basically unaffected—or we can journey with Jesus to his cross, as partakers of and participants in his passion. It all depends on what we choose to *set our faces toward.* What will it be?

Pray: Ask God how he desires you to participate in this journey to the cross rather than simply being a bystander or an onlooker. Ask him what your cross might be, and how you must die in order that you might be raised to new life.

Closing Prayer: Thank you, Lord Jesus, for *setting your face* to go to Jerusalem. Thank you for being willing to pay the high cost for my sinfulness. Give me the courage during this season to travel alongside you on your journey to the cross, that I might more fully understand both the depths of my sin and the depths of your love. I pray in your Holy Name. Amen.

Saturday

Come to Stillness: Spend a few minutes in silence before God, just being with him. He is always present to you, just allow yourself to be fully present to him.

Opening Prayer: Lord Jesus, help me to be willing to follow you no matter where it may lead, no matter what it might cost, no matter what I must leave behind. Amen.

Scripture: Luke 9:57-62

As they were going along the road, someone said to him, "I will follow you wherever you go." And Jesus said to him, "Foxes have holes, and birds of the air have nests, but the Son of Man has nowhere to lay his head." To another he said, "Follow me." But he said, "Lord, let me first go and bury my father." And Jesus said to him, "Leave the dead to bury their own dead. But as for you, go and proclaim the kingdom of God." Yet another said, "I will follow you, Lord, but let me first say farewell to those at my home." Jesus said to him, "No one who puts his hand to the plow and looks back is fit for the kingdom of God." (ESV)

Journal: To which of these three persons do you most relate? Why?

Which one speaks to something in your life these days? Why or how?

What word does Jesus have for you right now in response to your situation?

Will you follow him?

Is there a *"but"* involved? What is it?

Reflection: A friend of mine always used to say, "Everybody's got a big ole *but!*" Which always made me laugh, until the truth of the saying began to sink in a little bit. At that point, I usually stopped laughing and began to realize that, for me anyway, it was oh so true. As a matter of fact, I didn't just have *a* big ole *but,* I had *lots* of big ole *buts.* I was — and unfortunately still am — filled with so many excuses, rationalizations, and reasons why I simply cannot drop everything and follow Jesus. I'm glad to know I am not alone.

In this passage, we encounter three different *buts.* One given by Jesus, as a warning, and the other two given by would-be followers as conditions of their willingness to follow him. And, as we can see clearly in the text, Jesus really isn't too keen on us trying to set the conditions by which we would be willing to follow him. With him it's either all or nothing.

The first *but* comes as a person approaches Jesus and says, "I will follow you wherever you go." An admirable statement, no doubt. But, when push came to shove, would it prove to be true? For the would-be follower doesn't realize what he or she is saying. Jesus, after all, is on the way to Jerusalem. What lies before him is rejection, suffering, and death. It is not a journey for the faint of heart and Jesus wants this dear one to fully realize that. "Are you ready to rough it?" Jesus says, "We're not staying in the best inns, you know." (Luke 9:58, *The Message*) For it is not an easy trip, this journey to the cross. It is likely to cost our very lives. Are we really ready for that?

The second *but* comes in response to the call of Jesus to another would-be follower to "Follow me." Which is interesting, because this statement of Jesus is an imperative, which doesn't generally invite discussion.

Jesus wasn't asking a question here. He wasn't offering an invitation. He was giving a command. And yet the reply he gets is one of negotiation: "*First,* let me go bury my father." *First.* It is an extremely telling word. One that Jesus saw right to the heart of. "Leave the dead to bury their own dead," Jesus said, "But as for you, go and proclaim the kingdom of God." There is no negotiation when it comes to following Jesus. We don't get the freedom or the discretion to decide what comes *first.* He comes first, regardless of what else we might try to put before him. It is a pretty radical statement, but then again, Jesus is pretty radical himself.

The final *but* comes when yet another would-be follower says to Jesus, "I will follow you, Lord, *but* let me first say farewell to those at my home." Again, another encounter with the word *first,* for what would appear to be yet another noble cause. I mean, surely Jesus would want us to say goodbye to our families, right? Is Jesus anti-family? Not at all, but Jesus is discerning. He is able to tell when anything in our lives comes before him. Anything!

Jesus knows that when we put our families before him, we have gotten our affections out of order. And when our affections are out of order they are not able to function the way they were designed to function. The truth is that we cannot possibly love our families well if we are not loving Jesus *first.* When we put our families before Jesus, we put them in a position they were never intended to occupy. They become the source of our life and our happiness. And when they become the source of our life and our happiness, we demand from them something only God can give us. Which makes loving them next to impossible, because we need them too much. And when we need them we cannot truly love them because we are constantly trying to manipulate, or extort, love from them. So Jesus is not anti-family, Jesus just knows that he must be first in order for us to love our families the way we were intended to.

That is what the season of Lent is all about: coming face to face with our *buts*, trying to determine what is occupying *first* place in our hearts and lives, and moving from would-be followers to absolute followers of Jesus. What would it look like for you to fully say "yes" to Jesus; no *ifs, ands,* or *buts*?

Pray: Spend some time in prayer, telling Jesus your response to his call to follow him.

Closing Prayer: Lord Jesus, give me the grace, the strength, and the courage to say a full and complete *yes* to your call to follow you. Take away all of my *buts* and fill me instead with a steadfast commitment to your direction for my life, whatever that may be, wherever that may lead. Amen.

First Sunday of Lent

Come to Stillness: Spend a few minutes in silence, allowing your heart and mind to become still and calm. It is very likely that when God finally speaks, he will do so in a whisper. Make sure your soul is quiet enough to hear him.

Opening Prayer: Father, thank you that as difficult as some days can be, we can always live with the assurance that somehow you are mysteriously using our struggles to mold us into your image, for your glory. May we always *set our hearts on pilgrimage,* whatever that may mean. May we fix our eyes firmly on you, rather than on the ever-changing circumstances around us. Amen.

Scripture: Psalm 84:5-7

What joy for those whose strength comes from the Lord, who have set their hearts on a pilgrimage to Jerusalem. When they walk through the Valley of Weeping, it will become a place of refreshing springs. The autumn rains will clothe it with blessings. They will continue to grow stronger, and each of them will appear before God in Jerusalem. (NLT)

Journal: What does *setting your heart on pilgrimage* look like for you these days?

What is your Valley of Weeping right now?

How might God turn it into a *place of springs*?

What is your deepest hope for this Lenten journey?

Reflection: The Lenten journey is very much a pilgrimage. It is a time where we, like Jesus, set our faces to go to Jerusalem. It is a journey to the cross, a journey that passes through the Valley of Weeping, but ultimately ends at the place of springs — a place of new life and of resurrection.

So what does it mean to *set our hearts* on pilgrimage? Does it simply mean to follow, wherever the hard and lonely path may lead, trusting that Jesus knows the way to life? Does it mean to embrace — rather than avoid or deny — the struggle, the pain, and the brokenness of the season, and of my own heart, knowing that this is the soil in which new life is born? Does it mean being stripped down to the core of who I really am, and who God really is, in order that I may become all that he desires me to be? Does it mean *putting off* the old and the false within me, in order to *put on* the new and the true? Does it mean the *death* of old patterns, habits and ways of thinking and being, in order that I might be renewed in the image of my Creator?

Or does it mean simply putting one foot in front of the other, as I willingly follow my Savior into a scary and vulnerable land — the land of denying myself, taking up my cross, and following him? If that is indeed what it means, then by all means, O Lord, *set my heart on pilgrimage*, just as you set your face to go to Jerusalem, in order that I may truly know you and truly love you.

Pray: Hold your journey before God in prayer today. See if he has anything he wants to say to you. Now search your heart and see what you really want to say to him.

Closing Prayer: Lord God, thank you that it is in the midst of my brokenness that you meet me and do something within me that could be done no other way. Thank you for loving me enough to break me, so that you can remake me, more and more into your image. In the name of your Son, Jesus, I pray. Amen.

Monday
The First Week of Lent

Come to Stillness: Be still and know that I am God. (Psalm 46:10)

Opening Prayer: Father, I know my wounded and broken places oh so well. At times they can consume me and keep me from being able to hear your voice. Help me to see my pain as an invitation to know you more intimately rather than a reason to doubt the goodness of your heart. Help me to know that through my pain you desire to accomplish something very good in me. In the name of Jesus. Amen.

Scripture: Isaiah 6:1-8

In the year that King Uzziah died, I saw the Lord sitting on a throne, high and lifted up, and the train of His *robe* filled the temple. Above it stood seraphim; each one had six wings: with two he covered his face, with two he covered his feet, and with two he flew. And one cried to another and said:

> "Holy, holy, holy *is* the Lord of hosts;
> The whole earth *is* full of His glory!"

And the posts of the door were shaken by the voice of him who cried out, and the house was filled with smoke. So I said:

> "Woe *is* me, for I am undone! Because I *am* a man
> of unclean lips, and I dwell in the midst of a people
> of unclean lips; for my eyes have seen the King,

The Lord of hosts."

Then one of the seraphim flew to me, having in his hand a live coal *which* he had taken with the tongs from the altar. And he touched my mouth *with it,* and said:

"Behold, this has touched your lips; your iniquity is taken away, and your sin purged."

Also I heard the voice of the Lord, saying:

"Whom shall I send, and who will go for Us?"

Then I said, "Here *am* I! Send me." (NKJV)

Journal: When was the last time you were *undone?* Why?

What effect did it have on you?

How did it change you?

How did God speak to you in the midst of that circumstance?

What do you think God is trying to accomplish in you this season? Does it in any way bring to mind the experience of being *undone*?

Reflection:

undone

years and years of hard work
diligently putting it all together
piece by piece
thinking all is well
progress is being made

but then you
come and scramble the whole picture
leaving pieces scattered everywhere

you smile lovingly
as i sit in the middle of the mess
knowing that i don't know
knowing that i'm undone
and thinking to yourself
now that's progress
~*The Blue Book* by Jim Branch

Pray: Ask God to give you eyes to see what he is up to in your life, even if it is chaotic and disruptive at times.

Closing Prayer: O Lord, our God, give us a way of seeing that goes far beyond our surroundings or circumstances; one that allows us to live our lives from the firm foundation of our belief in your deep love and care for us; one that is totally convinced of both your sovereignty and your affection. In the name of Jesus. Amen.

Tuesday
The First Week of Lent

Come to Stillness: Spend a few minutes in silence and allow your soul to come to rest. This will make fruitful space within you for God to move and to act.

Opening Prayer: Lord God, there are so many times and so many places in my heart and life where I am still resistant to you and unwilling to let you have your way with me. I am unwilling to follow you to uncomfortable or unknown places. I am unwilling to set aside my own convenience and comfort to embrace your desire and direction for my life. I am unwilling to let go of the many things, patterns, and agendas I am constantly pursuing in order to fully pursue you. O Lord, forgive me for my unwillingness. Change my heart. Lord, have mercy! Amen.

Scripture Reading: Luke 13:31-35

At that very hour some Pharisees came and said to him, "Get away from here, for Herod wants to kill you." And he said to them, "Go and tell that fox, 'Behold, I cast out demons and perform cures today and tomorrow, and the third day I finish my course. Nevertheless, I must go on my way today and tomorrow and the day following, for it cannot be that a prophet should perish away from Jerusalem.' O Jerusalem, Jerusalem, the city that kills the prophets and stones those who are sent to it! How often would I have gathered your children together as a hen gathers her brood under her wings, and you were not willing! Behold, your house is forsaken. And I tell you, you will not see me until you

say, 'Blessed is he who comes in the name of the Lord!'"
(ESV)

Journal: What word best describes your spirit these
days, as far as life with God is concerned: *willing* or
unwilling?

Why does that word describe your response to God?

Where in your life with God are you *unwilling* these
days?

How might God desire to gather you under his wings?

Are you willing?

Reflection: I have come to the conclusion that I live a lot of my spiritual life in simple unwillingness. There are so many beautiful things that God wants to do with me and within me but, for some strange reason, I am just downright resistant. The reason for that resistance seems to be that I am simply too full of myself: my needs, my wants, my agendas, my plans, my pursuits, or, in other words, my will. Somehow, instead of "*Thy will be done*," my mantra has become "*My will be done*." So maybe a better word than *unwilling* is *willful* — as in being full of my own will.

The bottom line seems to be that I am simply too full of myself; for when I am willful I am unwilling to follow anyone's agenda or direction but my own. It is a dark and ugly truth that I typically come face to face with during this time of year. The time of year when we hear a weeping Jesus, heading toward the cross, asking us why we would not be willing to let him gather us under his loving and protective wings. Lord, have mercy.

Pray: Spend some time before God lifting up those areas of your life and faith where you are simply *unwilling*.

Closing Prayer: Lord Jesus, capture my heart during this season with the depths of your love and mercy. Empty me of all my unwillingness and make me wholly yours. Have mercy on me, O Lord. Amen.

Wednesday
The First Week of Lent

Come to Stillness: Spend a few minutes before God in silence, preparing your heart for whatever he might have for you today.

Opening Prayer: Lord God, open my ears to hear you this day. And cause me to truly listen to what you have to say, even if it is a difficult and challenging thing to hear. Amen.

Scripture Reading: Ezekiel 3:1-11

And he said to me, "Son of man, eat whatever you find here. Eat this scroll, and go, speak to the house of Israel." So I opened my mouth, and he gave me this scroll to eat. And he said to me, "Son of man, feed your belly with this scroll that I give you and fill your stomach with it." Then I ate it, and it was in my mouth as sweet as honey.

And he said to me, "Son of man, go to the house of Israel and speak with my words to them. For you are not sent to a people of foreign speech and a hard language, but to the house of Israel—not to many peoples of foreign speech and a hard language, whose words you cannot understand. Surely, if I sent you to such, they would listen to you. But the house of Israel will not be willing to listen to you, for they are not willing to listen to me: because all the house of Israel have a hard forehead and a stubborn heart. Behold, I have made your face as hard as their faces, and your forehead as hard as their foreheads. Like emery harder than flint have I made your forehead. Fear them not, nor be dismayed at their looks, for they are a rebellious house." Moreover, he said to me, "Son of man, all my words that I shall speak to you receive in your heart, and hear with your ears. And go to the exiles, to your people, and speak to them and say to them, 'Thus says the Lord God,' whether they hear or refuse to hear." (ESV)

Journal: What do you think God wants to say to you today?

Are you willing or unwilling to listen?

Is there something difficult or disruptive that he needs to address within you? What is it?

Are you willing to receive it?

Where in your life right now are you *hard headed* or *stubborn hearted*?

Reflection: The journey through Lent is a difficult one. It involves coming face to face with things we would rather not see, and hearing truths we would rather not hear. It is like someone showing us a picture of ourselves that is exceedingly unflattering; and, unfortunately, there is no delete button to hit so we can wipe it all away.

I don't know about you, but I am not usually good at hearing the hard truth about myself. In fact, I go to great lengths to avoid it, and try to make sure that no one else will be able to uncover it either. Sometimes I do this by going on offense; spending my time and energy making my case, trying to convince myself and my world that the truth about me is not so ugly after all. And sometimes I do this by going on defense; trying to avoid or escape or deny the truth by rationalizing, comparing, medicating, or running away into extreme activity or busyness. One of my "go to" strategies when I have hard, unpleasant truth about myself that I need to face is to race off into my world to manipulate affirmation out of anyone and everyone I meet. It is pathetic, really.

But God loves us far too much to allow us to get away with that for long. At some point he comes into our lives and speaks with such clarity that the truth simply becomes unavoidable. At that painful moment, we must realize that God's intent is always love, making us into the people he desires us to be. Anything less than his creation-intent for us will not do. So he comes and he speaks. And, if we are wise and courageous, we will listen and heed. Because the hard things that he might have to say will always lead us to what we most deeply desire—freedom, joy, and peace. And the very taste of those things will be *as sweet as honey in our mouths*. Thanks be to God!

Pray: Talk with God today about the *hard things* he is saying in your life and in your heart.

Closing Prayer: Lord Jesus, in this first week of Lent, give us the courage and the strength to fully face both our sinfulness and our great need of your mercy and grace. May these next days and weeks help us to see both the high cost of our sin and the unfathomable depths of your love. Amen.

Thursday
The First Week of Lent

Come to Stillness: Take a few minutes and be still and quiet, allowing your heart and your mind to slow down. This will create fruitful space for you to be with God today.

Opening Prayer: O Holy God, apart from you we are totally lost, full of sin, and without hope. Help us to see the gravity of our predicament, so that we might be overwhelmed by the depths of your love. In the name of your Son, our Savior, Jesus we pray. Amen.

Scripture Reading: Romans 3:9-18

What then? Are we Jews any better off? No, not at all. For we have already charged that all, both Jews and Greeks, are under sin, as it is written:
"None is righteous, no, not one;
no one understands;
no one seeks for God.
All have turned aside; together they have become worthless;
no one does good,
not even one."
"Their throat is an open grave;
they use their tongues to deceive."
"The venom of asps is under their lips."
"Their mouth is full of curses and bitterness."
"Their feet are swift to shed blood;
in their paths are ruin and misery,
and the way of peace they have not known."
"There is no fear of God before their eyes." (ESV)

Journal: What response comes up within you as you read the scripture for today?

Is there any word or image that seems to stand out? Why?

Pay attention to that word or image and see what God has to say to you through it.

Reflection: What could possibly be the value of reflecting upon and meditating upon words as dismal and depressing as those in Romans 3:9-18? A wise man once said that we can never know how unbelievably wonderful the Good News is until we fully understand how terribly awful the bad news is. In other words, we can't possibly know the true beauty of the Light until we have wrestled with the ugliness of our own inner darkness. We must have the courage to face the depths of our depravity before we can fully understand and appreciate the immense beauty of God's goodness and his love.

That is why we must embrace the hard words of Romans 3 rather than trying to deny them or escape them by running too quickly to the cross. First we must fully understand the whole reason why the cross is necessary. When we truly embrace these words of scripture, we begin to see the enormous chasm between sinful man and a holy God; a divide that ironically seems only to grow wider the older and wiser we get, and the closer we get to Jesus. Because as our knowledge of God grows larger, the distance between the two of us seems to grow as well, and the more we realize our enormous need for a Savior. But as the gap between us grows bigger, so does the cross. The cross is big enough to bridge any gap. In fact, the cross is bigger than we ever dared to dream. So, in an odd but necessary sort of way, the more aware we become of our own sinfulness, the more aware we become of the enormity of his great love.

Pray: Acknowledge your great need for God's mercy today. And celebrate his gracious forgiveness in Christ.

Closing Prayer: O Saving God, thank you that though our sin is deep, your love is deeper still. Thank you that your cross is always larger and more beautiful than we could ever imagine. Hallelujah!

Friday
First Week of Lent

Come to Stillness: Spend a few minutes before God in silent prayer. Set your heart and your mind on him and allow the tensions and distractions of the day to melt away. Set your attention fully on him and see what he has to say to you today.

Opening Prayer: Thank you, Lord Jesus, that while we were yet sinners, powerless to do anything about our spiritual condition, you demonstrated your love for us by dying in our place. O how deep the love that would make the God of all creation become a lowly man in order to die a death that we rightly deserve. Thank you, Lord Jesus, thank you!

Scripture: Romans 5:6-8

You see, at just the right time, when we were still powerless, Christ died for the ungodly. Very rarely will anyone die for a righteous person, though for a good person someone might possibly dare to die. But God demonstrates his own love for us in this: While we were still sinners, Christ died for us. (NIV)

Journal: What do the words of today's scripture do within you?

How aware are you today of your own sinfulness?

How aware are you of God's great love?

What is your response to his love today?

Reflection: *While we were still sinners.* The Greek word here for *sinner* is *hamartōlos,* which comes from the root *hamartanō,* meaning *to miss the mark.* We are people who are constantly missing the mark. Have you missed the mark recently? What did that look like? What did it feel like? Do you ever feel like, regardless of what you do, you just can't measure up? I feel that way a lot. Probably because, apart from the saving work of Jesus, that is the condition of my heart and soul. It is a condition that runs so deep that, this side of heaven, I'm not sure I will ever be completely free of it.

That's the picture that we are offered here in Romans 5. But luckily that is not where the picture ends. Thanks be to God that even though we fall woefully short (and woefully is not nearly a strong enough word) of what we were created to be — again and again and again — God still chooses to demonstrate his great love for us by sending Jesus to die. God took our mess on himself, so that we might be made whole and clean. That should make us glad. That should give us hope. And that should also make us humble, constantly reminding us that it was because of our mess that Jesus had to get his hands dirty in the first place.

The good news is that Jesus never seemed to be afraid to get his hands dirty. No mess was too big for him. He was constantly touching lepers and receiving kisses from prostitutes for heaven's sake. So if he was okay with getting his hands messy, shouldn't we be also? Yet, oftentimes we demand that people be mess-free before we will have anything to do with them. I'm so glad Jesus was not like that. In fact, it was while we were still a mess that he died for us. That is not a license to continue to live in our messiness, but a reminder that, whether we are aware of it or not, we are all still a mess apart from God's grace. Therefore, if we are going to be like Jesus, we can never demand that everyone we meet be mess-free before we will have anything to do with them. Nor can anyone demand that we be mess-free. Jesus does not.

My guess is that none of us has finished making a mess of our lives, there are still plenty of opportunities ahead. The reality is that life is simply messy sometimes. That does not mean that we should ever set out in the direction of messy, we are called to much greater things than that—holiness and righteousness. But it does mean that when messes occur, all is not lost. Because it is in the middle of the messes —*while we were yet sinners*—that God demonstrates his great love.

Pray: Give thanks to God, this day, for his amazing grace.

Closing Prayer: Lord Jesus Christ, have mercy on me, a sinner!

Saturday
First Week of Lent

Come to Stillness: Take a few minutes in silence to clear your mind and heart. Let go of anything that might be distracting you, consuming you, or weighing you down. Focus your attention on God and his presence with you, and within you, at this moment. Be free to simply be with him. There is nothing to prove, nothing to earn, nothing to achieve.

Opening Prayer: O Christ Jesus; when all is darkness and we feel our weakness and helplessness, give us the sense of Your presence, Your love, Your strength. Help us to have perfect trust in Your protecting love and strengthening power, so that nothing may frighten or worry us, for, living close to You, we shall see Your hand, Your purpose, Your will through all things. Amen. ~St. Ignatius of Loyola

Scripture: Romans 3:21-26

But now the righteousness of God has been manifested apart from the law, although the Law and the Prophets bear witness to it—the righteousness of God through faith in Jesus Christ for all who believe. For there is no distinction: for all have sinned and fall short of the glory of God, and are justified by his grace as a gift, through the redemption that is in Christ Jesus, whom God put forward as a propitiation by his blood, to be received by faith. This was to show God's righteousness, because in his divine forbearance he had passed over former sins. It was to show his righteousness at the present time, so that he might be just and the justifier of the one who has faith in Jesus. (ESV)

Journal: How do you try to justify your own existence?

How do you respond to the fact that you are justified freely in Christ?

Reflection: Do you ever find yourself trying to *justify your existence?* When I read this phrase the other day, it simply stopped me in my tracks. Because I do that all the time. In fact, most of the things I do in my life are nothing more than feeble attempts to justify my own existence.

It reminds me of a line from that old classic movie *Chariots of Fire* where one of the characters, Harold Abrams, is asked about his upcoming race and he says, "*And now in one hour's time, I will be out there again. I will raise my eyes and look down that corridor; four feet wide, with ten lonely seconds to justify my existence. But will I?*" What a powerful, incredibly haunting, line. You can hear and feel the very weight of the world squarely on his shoulders. It is simply too much for one person to bear.

Justifying my existence doesn't involve running in the Olympics, but that doesn't make it feel like any less a burden. I live daily with the idea in my head that I am "not enough" and can never "measure up." It is an idea that has grown in me and taken root deep in my heart and soul. It is an idea whose roots run so deep that it is incredibly difficult to uproot them completely. And it significantly affects the way I go about living my life; constantly pushing me to try and prove to myself, and to my world, that I am worth loving. To convince myself that what I have to contribute is important. I don't know about you, but I constantly feel the need to prove to the world that the work that I do, that the ministry I have, that the gifts I possess, are necessary and significant. It tends to keep me running breathlessly about, and can be both overwhelming and exhausting at times.

But Jesus calls me to live out of another voice altogether. For he has given me all of the justification my life will ever need. I am fully and freely justified in him. His love defines me. His deep affection gives me my value and worth, so that I don't have to run around looking for someone or something to justify my existence. He alone does that. He alone can give me freedom; freedom to be loved and, more importantly, freedom to love. I can genuinely love his world because I do not need anything (affirmation, attention, importance) from his world. I think that is why the main character in *Chariots of Fire*, Eric Liddell, when asked why he ran, was able to answer beautifully, I run because "when I run I feel his pleasure." May it be the same for each of us.

Pray: Write a letter to God today, thanking him for his free gift of justification.

Closing Prayer: Lord Jesus, help me to live in the fullness of the freedom you have provided; the freedom from having to justify myself — my life, my existence, my work, my worth. Thank you that justification is a free gift from you, the fruit of your love and obedience. You have taken away my sin and have given me your righteousness. All that you have, you give to me. Thanks be to God!

Second Sunday of Lent

Come to Stillness: Take a few minutes of silence to make room within you for God to speak and to move.

Opening Prayer: Late have I loved you, O Beauty, so ancient and so new, late have I loved you! And behold, you were within me and I was outside, and there I sought for you, and in my deformity I rushed headlong into the well-formed things that you have made. You were with me, and I was not with you. ~St. Augustine

Scripture: Genesis 32:22-31

The same night he arose and took his two wives, his two female servants, and his eleven children, and crossed the ford of the Jabbok. He took them and sent them across the stream, and everything else that he had. And Jacob was left alone. And a man wrestled with him until the breaking of the day. When the man saw that he did not prevail against Jacob, he touched his hip socket, and Jacob's hip was put out of joint as he wrestled with him. Then he said, "Let me go, for the day has broken." But Jacob said, "I will not let you go unless you bless me." And he said to him, "What is your name?" And he said, "Jacob." Then he said, "Your name shall no longer be called Jacob, but Israel, for you have striven with God and with men, and have prevailed." Then Jacob asked him, "Please tell me your name." But he said, "Why is it that you ask my name?" And there he blessed him. So Jacob called the name of the place Peniel, saying, "For I have seen God face to face, and yet my life has been delivered." The sun rose upon him as he passed Penuel, limping because of his hip. (ESV)

Journal: What, or who, are you wrestling with these days?

How are you wrestling with God?

What is he doing in you as a result?

Reflection: I have a suspicion that at least part of what needs to happen within me during the season of Lent has something to do with God wrestling away the *old* in me in order to make way for the *new*. It's almost like I am stuck in a decaying orbit and have no hope of breaking free from the gravitational pull that keeps me bound to it, unless I am liberated by Someone much larger than myself. Someone who can set me free from my *old* ways of being and of seeing, in order that I might live my life more fully the way he intended me to. The problem is that the way to this *new* life of freedom and wholeness leads through *a wrestling* that is likely to leave me—as it did Jacob—wounded and broken first. Yet that path seems the only way to the new life and the new (true) identity I most desperately long for. So, unfortunately, the wrestling can't be avoided or bypassed.

Thomas Merton said it so well when he said that: "Only this inner rending, the tearing of the heart, brings this joy. It lets out our sins, and lets in the clean air of God's spring, the sunlight of the days that advance toward Easter. Rending of garments lets in nothing but the cold. The rending of heart is that tearing away from ourselves and our *vetustas*—the *oldness* of the old man, wearied with the boredom and drudgery of an indifferent existence, that we may turn to God and taste His mercy, in the liberty of His sons."

There is a wounding in this wrestling that is intended to make way for something *new* to be born. So the struggle, albeit frightening and uncomfortable, is a glorious necessity in the process of being made whole. I cannot do it on my own (heaven knows I've tried), only God can give me the power to break free from the *tired* and the *old*, and step into the *fresh* and the *new*.

The tricky part is that we, like Jacob, don't always realize right off the bat that we're actually wrestling with God. At first Jacob thought he was just wrestling with *a man*. It wasn't until later — new name and all — that he finally recognized that it was, indeed, God he was wrestling with. The same is true for me. At times I think I am wrestling with my anxieties or my insecurity, or that I am wrestling with a person with whom I am in conflict. At times I think I am wrestling with my own circumstances, or my church, or my spouse, or my vocation. At times I think I am wrestling with motivation, or frustration, or discontent. And if I look closely beneath each one of those things, I will recognize that the *man behind the curtain*, the one I'm really wrestling with, is God.

And when I discover this, it changes everything. I realize that it is not just about my pain, or my struggle, or my death, but it is always about my life. I realize that it is not my circumstances, or my relationships, or the people in my world that need to change, it is me. *God* is wrestling with *me*, trying to accomplish something deep in my soul. Something that will change everything about me, the same way it did with Jacob.

Pray: Wrestle with God today in prayer, whatever that may look like.

Closing Prayer: O God, give me eyes to see that it is *you* who is at work in my life behind all of the struggles, conflicts, and circumstances. You are the one I am truly wrestling with. For you are trying to accomplish something good and beautiful in me that only this type of wrestling can accomplish. You are trying to strip away all of the old — old names and old patterns — in order that I might receive the new. Thank you!

Monday
Second Week of Lent

Come to Stillness: Spend a few minutes in silence quieting your heart, so that you might be able to hear the voice of the Father telling you how much he delights in you.

Opening Prayer: Lord God, our heavenly Father, may we always remember that we are your beloved children, and may that knowledge give us the strength and the power and the encouragement we need to be victorious over temptation. Amen.

Scripture: Matthew 3:13-4:11

Then Jesus came from Galilee to the Jordan to John, to be baptized by him. John would have prevented him, saying, "I need to be baptized by you, and do you come to me?" But Jesus answered him, "Let it be so now, for thus it is fitting for us to fulfill all righteousness." Then he consented. And when Jesus was baptized, immediately he went up from the water, and behold, the heavens were opened to him, and he saw the Spirit of God descending like a dove and coming to rest on him; and behold, a voice from heaven said, "This is my beloved Son, with whom I am well pleased."

Then Jesus was led up by the Spirit into the wilderness to be tempted by the devil. And after fasting forty days and forty nights, he was hungry. And the tempter came and said to him, "If you are the Son of God, command these stones to become loaves of bread." But he answered, "It is written,

"'Man shall not live by bread alone,
   but by every word that comes from the mouth of
   God.'"
Then the devil took him to the holy city and set him
on the pinnacle of the temple and said to him, "If you
are the Son of God, throw yourself down, for it is
written,
   "'He will command his angels concerning you,'
And
   "'On their hands they will bear you up,
   lest you strike your foot against a stone.'"
Jesus said to him, "Again it is written, 'You shall not
put the Lord your God to the test.'" Again, the devil
took him to a very high mountain and showed him all
the kingdoms of the world and their glory. And he said
to him, "All these I will give you, if you will fall down
and worship me." Then Jesus said to him, "Be gone,
Satan! For it is written,
   "'You shall worship the Lord your God
   and him only shall you serve.'"
Then the devil left him, and behold, angels came and
were ministering to him. (ESV)

Journal: What words did God want ringing in the ears
of his Son as he spent forty days in the desert being
tempted by the devil?

Why do you think God gave Jesus those particular words?

How do those same words help you to fight temptation in your own life?

Reflection: Don't you just love the fact that the words the Father wanted ringing in the ears of his Son as he battled for forty days in the wilderness were, "You are my son, whom I love. With you I am well pleased." Obviously God knew that one of the chief strategies of the enemy is to try to make us doubt who we really are. In fact, that's how the devil begins his first two temptations: "If you really are God's son..." For he knows that if he can forge any such doubt at all in our hearts, he has begun to develop a foothold. Therefore, the Father took care of that well in advance with Jesus. The Father wanted Jesus to know at the very core of his being that he was God's Beloved Son. Those words were the very bread Jesus fed on for all of his days and nights in the desert. Those words nourished and sustained his soul.

I don't know about you, but I find that my identity is a place where I am often attacked as well. It is a very vulnerable area for me. You see, unlike Jesus, I have trouble really believing that God could ever love someone like me. So it doesn't take much of an attack for doubt to begin to creep into my heart and mind. That's why I constantly need to be attentive to the voice of the Father. I desperately need to hear his words of delight and affection over and over again before I can believe that they are actually true. Unfortunately, I am easy prey for doubt and insecurity and self-contempt. Therefore, I need constant reminders. For when I am finally able to believe it is really true, and to fully trust who I really am to God and in God, I have strength and courage to face the temptations of the day.

Pray: Listen to the voice that calls you beloved.

Closing Prayer: Help us, Lord Jesus. Help us to see temptation for what it is. Help us to be attentive to all of the ways we are tempted to believe that you do not really care for us. Help us to recognize the ways in which we are demanding and manipulative of you. Give us the grace and the strength and the wisdom to respond to these temptations as you did. Lord, have mercy. Christ, have mercy. Amen.

Tuesday
Second Week of Lent

Come to Stillness: Be still and silent before God for a few minutes. Come to him with no demands and no expectations. Just come to be with him — that will produce fertile soil in your soul.

Opening Prayer: Lord God, help us to believe that you are able to bring life out of the most painful, chaotic, and messy circumstances. When we are tempted to doubt the goodness of your heart, or to lose hope that you will, indeed, care for us, help us to hold fast to an undying trust in your unfailing love. In the name of Jesus. Amen.

Scripture: John 11:38-44

Then Jesus, deeply moved again, came to the tomb. It was a cave, and a stone lay against it. Jesus said, "Take away the stone." Martha, the sister of the dead man, said to him, "Lord, by this time there will be an odor, for he has been dead four days." Jesus said to her, "Did I not tell you that if you believed you would see the glory of God?" So they took away the stone. And Jesus lifted up his eyes and said, "Father, I thank you that you have heard me. I knew that you always hear me, but I said this on account of the people standing around, that they may believe that you sent me." When he had said these things, he cried out with a loud voice, "Lazarus, come out." The man who had died came out, his hands and feet bound with linen strips, and his face wrapped with a cloth. Jesus said to them, "Unbind him, and let him go." (ESV)

Journal: Where have the circumstances of your life made it difficult for you to believe in God's heart?

Who can you relate to most in this story? Why?

What stones do you need rolled away within you these days?

Reflection: The cave is dark and cold, filled with death and decay. *After all, it's been four days since the dead man was placed inside. There's no more hope; that's it! Death has had the final word. If only Jesus would've shown up sooner, but now what could he possibly do?* Ever feel that way? Ever feel like all hope is lost; like life and health and change are not possible because of the gravitational pull of the deadness inside? Martha would have us believe that it is just too late. "Don't open up that tomb, it's going to stink. It is far too messy to be redeemed." I'm so glad that Jesus didn't share her sentiments. And I'm glad that he still doesn't. In fact, Jesus specializes in messy. That's because Jesus knows that for something (or someone) to be resurrected it has to die first. Why do you think he waited four days before he arrived at the tomb? Why do you think he said to Martha, "*Did I not tell you that if you believed you would see the glory of God?*" You see, Jesus is bigger than death; be it the death of someone we love, the death of a relationship we hold near and dear, the death of a dream, or the death that lives within us on a regular basis. Death would have you believe that *this is it. That's all there is. There's no way out of this pain and darkness and depression. You are stuck. You are trapped. Life can never be the same again.* But Jesus knows better. Maybe that's why he weeps. Maybe he is heartbroken that somewhere deep inside, we don't truly believe that he can redeem *this,* whatever *this* may be. Maybe he is weeping over the fact that we do not really believe that he can, or will, bring life out of our unimaginable pain and brokenness. Maybe his tears come from the fact that our circumstances have made us doubt the goodness of his heart. And maybe his sadness is somehow related to our *stuckness.* Who knows?

Luckily the story doesn't end there. In fact, Jesus then calls out, *"Take away the stone."* And some unknown, unseen (to us) group of people springs into action. People who are filled with the hope that this is not, in fact, the end. People who are filled with the faith to know that even though things look unredeemable, Jesus is able to breathe life into even the most dismal and hopeless and painful of circumstances. People who care so deeply for the one inside the tomb that they are standing by, willing and ready to do whatever it takes to help make that redemption possible. "He can't get out of the tomb by himself," they think, "so why don't we help roll the stone away and just see what Jesus will do?"

Truth be told, there can never be enough stone-rollers in the world. In fact, what if that was what our churches were full of? Oh what a different world it would be! Because stone-rollers don't care about the stink. They don't care about the mess. They don't care about what anyone thinks. They are beyond all of that, because at some point in time someone had the courage and the grace to roll their stone away, so that they might walk out of the grave into the light of new life. And because of that, if there's ever a time when someone needs a stone to be rolled away (rather than to be avoided, or judged, or given up on) they want to be the first in line. They want to be the ones to spring into action whenever Jesus utters the words, "Take the stone away." Being a stone-roller is a beautiful, beautiful thing.

After the stone is rolled away, Jesus turns his eyes, and his heart, to his Father — the giver of all life. He knows the Father's heart like no one else. He knows the goodness, he knows the faithfulness, he knows the love, and he knows that those standing around — particularly the family of this dead man — are doubting all of that at the moment.

Maybe, somehow, they think that it was God's hand that caused all of this pain, but Jesus knows better. He knows the heart of the Father that groans for (and with) his creation (Romans 8:26) in their most broken hours, so he prays. He prays that *they* might *believe*; believe that he is the God of life even in the face of death, believe that *they* can trust his heart even when they can't see his hand, believe that he was sent from the Father's side to redeem the unredeemable.

So Jesus calls out the dead man's name and tells him to *come out*. Notice he doesn't just say *Come alive,* or *Be healed,* but *Come out.* Because a significant part of the new life that Jesus calls us to is about leaving the tomb behind. He raises us from the dead, breathes new life into our souls, and then calls each of us to *"Come out."* In fact, being raised to life again and yet choosing to remain in the tomb is not an option, even though so many people live like it is. So many people, claiming to belong to Jesus, claiming to have been raised from the dead, are still sitting in the darkness of the tomb of shame or guilt or anger or bitterness or unforgiveness or self-pity. They are still living a life that is anything but alive. They *must* take that step out of the tomb. Then, and only then, can the body of Christ (maybe even the same ones who rolled away the stone) come alongside them and help take off the grave clothes, so that they can be totally alive and totally free.

Pray: Lift your pain up to God today. Allow him to comfort you and give you his peace.

Closing Prayer: O Jesus, help us to truly believe. Help us to believe that you are, indeed, the Resurrection and the Life. For if we truly believe it, then we will live like we truly believe it. Amen.

Wednesday
Second Week of Lent

Come to Stillness: Spend a few minutes before God in silence. Allow it to create some good, receptive soil in your soul for whatever he may desire to plant there today.

Opening Prayer: Lord God, be the delight of our hearts, even as we are the delight of yours. And help us to leave behind all thoughts, actions, and attitudes that do not reflect the beauty of that delight. May everything else pale in comparison with the passion we have to be truly yours. In the name of Jesus. Amen.

Scripture Reading: Isaiah 30:15-18

For thus said the Lord God, the Holy One of Israel,
"In returning and rest you shall be saved;
   in quietness and in trust shall be your strength."
But you were unwilling, and you said,
"No! We will flee upon horses";
   therefore you shall flee away;
and, "We will ride upon swift steeds";
   therefore your pursuers shall be swift.
A thousand shall flee at the threat of one;
   at the threat of five you shall flee,
till you are left
   like a flagstaff on the top of a mountain,
   like a signal on a hill.
Therefore the Lord waits to be gracious to you,
   and therefore he exalts himself to show mercy to you.
For the Lord is a God of justice;
   blessed are all those who wait for him. (ESV)

Journal: Why do you think someone might be resistant to the first lines of today's scripture reading?

Is there something in you today that is resistant to them?

Why do you think *returning, rest, quietness, and trust* are things that are so hard for us to do?

Are they hard for you?

Are they a significant part of your life and world? Why or why not?

Reflection: Letting go is hard. And it doesn't really matter what you are trying to let go of. In fact, letting go is so hard that most of us are simply unwilling (or unable) to do it, even if God is the one asking us to do so. Letting go is especially hard when the stakes are high; when what we are being asked to let go of is control, or agenda, or security, or significance. Then it is darn near impossible. For letting go is all about trust. It is about surrender. And ultimately it is about willingness.

Letting go forces us to answer some hard questions. Are we willing to put ourselves completely in God's hands? Are we willing to trust ourselves—and our families, or our finances, or our reputations—completely to God's care? Are we willing to stop calling all the shots and let him be the one who does that from now on?

Or are we simply unwilling? Are we unwilling to follow wherever he may lead? Are we unwilling to surrender all in pursuit of him alone? Are we unwilling to order our lives according to his will and his word?

Where is God asking you to let go today? Where is he asking you to be willing? Are you?

Pray: Ask God to show you today the places of willingness and unwillingness in your life.

Closing Prayer: Take, Lord, and receive all that I am and have. You've given it all to me; I give it all back to you. Do with me as you want. Just give me your love and your grace and that's enough. ~St. Ignatius

Thursday
Second Week of Lent

Come to Stillness: Sit in silence before God. Allow the voices around you and within you to quiet. Now listen for his still, small voice.

Opening Prayer: O gracious and Holy Father, give us wisdom to perceive you, diligence to seek you, patience to wait for you, eyes to behold you, a heart to meditate upon you, and a life to proclaim you; through the power of the Spirit of Jesus Christ our Lord. ~Saint Benedict

Scripture: Matthew 7:13-14

"Enter by the narrow gate. For the gate is wide and the way is easy that leads to destruction, and those who enter by it are many. For the gate is narrow and the way is hard that leads to life, and those who find it are few." (ESV)

Journal: Where in life right now are you choosing the easy way?

What would it look like to choose the hard way instead?

How have you recently seen the hard way lead to life?

Reflection: It's amazing how addicted I've become to ease. And it's even more amazing how that addiction doesn't seem to alarm me the way it should. Maybe that's why this reminder from Matthew is so helpful. It reminds me that if ease is my number one goal and pursuit—be it in my marriage, or my friendships, or my job, or my parenting, or my ministry, or even in my spiritual journey—then I are heading toward destruction. Oh maybe not destruction in the "eternal destination" sense of the word. After all, I've entered by the narrow gate, right?

This is a much more subtle type of destruction. This type of destruction involves the slow disintegration of the things I hold most dear. Be it the destruction of my marriage, or my friendships, or my community, or even my very soul. If I am constantly choosing the easy way rather than the hard way then I am never pressing past what is easiest to get to what is best. And what is best is seldom, if ever, easy.

Why do I tend to *settle* for what is easiest rather than pursuing what is best? Why do I continually settle for less than all God has for me and all he desires me to become? For it is the hard way that leads to life. It is the choice to constantly be engaging others rather than sitting back. It is the choice to constantly be moving toward those in my life and world rather than retreating in fear or apathy. It is the choice to drop the mask and come out of hiding rather than continuing to pretend, act, and perform. It is the choice to continually be vulnerable, genuine, and honest rather than to opt for shallowness, fearfulness, and self-protection. It is the choice to continually be willing to risk rather than always playing it safe. The choice to continually seek to love rather than to manipulate. All of this is hard, yet it is the hard way that *leads to life*.

So the choice before me today is to choose one or the other — the easy way or the hard way. And although the easy way might seem more attractive in the short run, it is hardly ever the best way in the grand scheme of eternity. Today, let us take the road less traveled. Let us enter by the narrow gate. Let us walk the harder, but much better, way. It is the way of Jesus. And it is the way to Jesus; the way, the truth, and the life.

Pray: Ask God to show you what choosing the *hard way that leads to life* looks like in your life right now.

Closing Prayer:
Lord,
The house of my soul is narrow;
enlarge it that you may enter in.
It is ruinous, O repair it!
It displeases Your sight.
I confess it, I know.
But who shall cleanse it,
to whom shall I cry but to you?
Cleanse me from my secret faults,
O Lord, and spare Your servant from strange sins.
~St. Augustine

Friday
Second Week of Lent

Come to Stillness: Spend a few minutes sitting before God in silence, allowing your heart and mind to come to rest. This will create good space within you to be attentive to his voice.

Opening Prayer: Most High, glorious God, enlighten the darkness of my heart, and give me right faith, certain hope, and perfect charity, wisdom and understanding, Lord, that I may carry out your holy and true command. Amen. ~St. Francis of Assisi

Scripture Reading: Mark 8:31-37

And he began to teach them that the Son of Man must suffer many things and be rejected by the elders and the chief priests and the scribes and be killed, and after three days rise again. And he said this plainly. And Peter took him aside and began to rebuke him. But turning and seeing his disciples, he rebuked Peter and said, "Get behind me, Satan! For you are not setting your mind on the things of God, but on the things of man."

And calling the crowd to him with his disciples, he said to them, "If anyone would come after me, let him deny himself and take up his cross and follow me. For whoever would save his life will lose it, but whoever loses his life for my sake and the gospel's will save it. For what does it profit a man to gain the whole world and forfeit his soul? For what can a man give in return for his soul? (ESV)

Journal: How does operating by your agenda get you in trouble sometimes?

In what areas of life is it most tempting to charge ahead before getting direction from God?

What would it look like for you to *have in mind the things of God,* rather than *having in mind the things of men?*

Are you willing to *get behind* Jesus?

Reflection: I don't know about you, but it is easy for me to get ahead of myself at times. To move and act and live life before I have really reflected and thought and prayed about the life I most want to live — or the life that God most wants to live in and through me.

And it is also easy in the life of faith to get ahead of God at times as well. It is easy for us to charge ahead with our own plans and schemes and agendas — even for the kingdom, mind you — without really listening and seeking and getting direction from God.

I'm glad to see that I am not alone. Peter had the same problem. So much so that when Jesus told him what was to come, Peter adamantly disagreed with him — even rebuked Jesus — because those plans did not agree with Peter's own agenda. That's where the "*Get behind me, Satan!*" part comes in. Peter had *charged ahead* when the place he needed to be was firmly *behind* — *behind Jesus*. And Jesus reminded him of that; quite boldly I might add.

It is just so easy to charge ahead sometimes; to follow our own plans for how we think things should work, or how we believe things should go, or how we want things to be. There is obviously a great danger when that happens. For when we charge ahead, we actually become *a stumbling block* to Jesus rather than a follower. For ours is not to charge ahead, ours is just to follow closely *behind*. What will that look like today?

Pray: Ask God to show you how you might be getting ahead of him these days, rather than following behind him.

Closing Prayer: O Lord, my God, forgive me when I have in mind the things of men rather than the things of God. Help me to be willing to embrace your direction and your will in all that I do, rather than my own. Amen.

Saturday
Second Week of Lent

Come to Stillness: Take a few minutes and sit before the Lord in silence. He longs to have both your attention and your affection. He longs to put his hands on you and heal you in ways, and in places, that will bring wholeness to your heart and soul.

Opening Prayer: Lord Jesus, thank you that you just couldn't stay away. Thank you that when you saw our plight and our struggle you came to walk among us. Thank you that when you saw our desperation and our pain and our need that you couldn't keep your hands to yourself. Thank you that you were — and still are — willing. Touch us in our places of deepest need. In your name and for your glory. Amen.

Scripture Read: Matthew 8:1-4

When Jesus came down from the mountainside, large crowds followed him. A man with leprosy came and knelt before him and said, "Lord, if you are willing, you can make me clean."

Jesus reached out his hand and touched the man. "I am willing," he said. "Be clean!" Immediately he was cleansed of his leprosy. Then Jesus said to him, "See that you don't tell anyone. But go, show yourself to the priest and offer the gift Moses commanded, as a testimony to them." (NIV)

Journal: How do you feel like the man with leprosy these days?

What does it say to you that Jesus was willing to reach out and touch him with his healing and cleansing touch?

Are there any parts of your life or heart that desperately need the healing or cleansing touch of the Savior?

Do you believe he is willing to touch you in those places?

Do you truly believe that he cares enough for you to do that?

Reflection: *"Lord, if you are willing…."* Does that phrase sound familiar to you? It certainly does to me. I'm glad to see that I am not the only who prays it. "Lord, if you are willing, you can take this difficult circumstance away. Lord, if you are willing you can heal this cancer. Lord, if you are willing you can reconcile this broken relationship. Lord, if you are willing, you can help me find the right job. Lord, if you are willing, you can provide for our financial needs. Lord, if you are willing, you can bring back my wayward child." The list is endless, it seems.

And the answer we get often seems to be different than the one given to the leprous man. But what we always need to remember is that Jesus is willing. Oh maybe he is not always willing to give us what we think we need or want at any given moment, but he is always willing to give us himself — which is ultimately what we need the most anyway. Even if he is not willing to *"take this cup from us"* whatever *this cup* may be, it is only because he has learned firsthand that ultimately God's will is the one most likely to move us in the direction of who he wants us to become.

He is always willing to form us more and more into his image — which is exactly what we were created for. He is always willing to draw near to us when we are brokenhearted. He is always willing to work out what is most in line with his glory, and our ultimate benefit in the long run (see Romans 8:28). And he is always willing to give us his love, which more than we could ever ask for or dream about, but which might come in a rather painful disguise from time to time. So whatever your circumstance, always remember: *He is willing.*

Pray: Lay the ugly areas of your life before God in prayer and ask him to reach out and touch those places, that you might be cleansed.

Closing Prayer: O Jesus, our Lord and Savior, thank you for your willingness, not only to touch and transform our ugliness, but to die on the cross for our sin. Thank you for your sacrifice. Thank you for your love. Thank you for the example you have given us to follow. Give us hearts that are as willing as yours. Amen.

Third Sunday of Lent

Come to Stillness: *Hear, O Israel.* That is one of God's greatest desires for us. Sit for a few minutes in silence and make that a real possibility.

Opening Prayer: O God, be the center of all of our affections, that we might love you above all else. For only then will our lives be ordered the way you created them to be. May you always be our first and our greatest affection, O God, both this day and every day. Amen.

Scripture: Deuteronomy 6:4-9

Hear, O Israel: The Lord our God, the Lord is one. Love the Lord your God with all your heart and with all your soul and with all your strength. These commandments that I give you today are to be on your hearts. Impress them on your children. Talk about them when you sit at home and when you walk along the road, when you lie down and when you get up. Tie them as symbols on your hands and bind them on your foreheads. Write them on the doorframes of your houses and on your gates. (NIV)

Journal: What consumes most of your thoughts and energy these days?

What does that tell you about the order of your affections?

Why is it important to order your affections?

What would it look like for God to be your greatest affection?

Reflection: God's ultimate desire is to be the greatest of all our affections, not just one among the many that constantly compete for the top spot in our hearts. For when we give ourselves to affections *lesser* than he, we rob him (the Great Affection) of his rightful place, and rob ourselves of the life that he intended for us.

The problem is that it is not always readily apparent—to us anyway—when something, or someone (even the good things of this life, like friends, family, ministry, etc.), has grabbed that top place that was intended only for him. When that happens, we become excessively attached to people, places, material possessions, occupations, titles, honors, achievements, and the acclaim or affirmation of others. These things are good in themselves when ordered and directed by the love of God. But they can become compulsions (or even addictions) and produce chaos when they replace God as the center of our lives and become essential to our happiness and identity.

Therefore, the saints of old made a practice of ruthless self-examination. They intentionally made time and space to listen to God and thus to constantly examine their affections to assure they were in proper order. We are wise to follow their lead. God must be first, before all else, for only then will we have the freedom to truly love others.

Pray: Love the Lord with all that is within you today in prayer. What do you want to say to him?

Closing Prayer: O Spirit of God. We ask you to help orient all our actions by your inspirations, carry them on by your gracious assistance, that every prayer and work of ours may always begin from you and through you be happily ended. Amen. ~*A Jesuit Prayer*

Monday
Third Week of Lent

Come to Stillness: Be still and know that he is God.

Opening Prayer: Lord God, help us to believe. Help us to believe that in all times and in all circumstances you will take care of us if we will simply trust you and follow you. Keep us, O Lord, from being unwilling to follow you because of fear; instead, help us to be willing to go wherever you may lead because of faith. In the name of your son, Jesus, we pray. Amen.

Scripture Reading: Deuteronomy 1:19-33

Then, as the Lord our God commanded us, we set out from Horeb and went toward the hill country of the Amorites through all that vast and dreadful wilderness that you have seen, and so we reached Kadesh Barnea. Then I said to you, "You have reached the hill country of the Amorites, which the Lord our God is giving us. See, the Lord your God has given you the land. Go up and take possession of it as the Lord, the God of your ancestors, told you. Do not be afraid; do not be discouraged."

Then all of you came to me and said, "Let us send men ahead to spy out the land for us and bring back a report about the route we are to take and the towns we will come to."

The idea seemed good to me; so I selected twelve of you, one man from each tribe. They left and went up into the hill country, and came to the Valley of Eshkol and explored it. Taking with them some of the fruit of the land, they brought it down to us and reported, "It is a good land that the Lord our God is giving us."

But you were unwilling to go up; you rebelled against the command of the Lord your God. You grumbled in your tents and said, "The Lord hates us; so he brought us out of Egypt to deliver us into the hands of the Amorites to destroy us. Where can we go? Our brothers have made our hearts melt in fear. They say, 'The people are stronger and taller than we are; the cities are large, with walls up to the sky. We even saw the Anakites there.'"

Then I said to you, "Do not be terrified; do not be afraid of them. The Lord your God, who is going before you, will fight for you, as he did for you in Egypt, before your very eyes, and in the wilderness. There you saw how the Lord your God carried you, as a father carries his son, all the way you went until you reached this place."

In spite of this, you did not trust in the Lord your God, who went ahead of you on your journey, in fire by night and in a cloud by day, to search out places for you to camp and to show you the way you should go. (NIV)

Journal: How does fear affect your level of willingness or unwillingness in your life with God?

Where are you unwilling to be obedient because you are afraid of what it might cost you?

What things seem like "giants" to you right now?

What things are scaring you away from what God has promised if you will just be willing and obedient?

Reflection: *Giants.* That is what the Israelites were afraid of. That is what kept them from taking possession of the land God had promised them, even though God had told them plainly that he would care for them and fight for them and give this *good* and fruitful land to them.

Not much has changed after all these years. We are still afraid of giants. Giants are still what keep us from taking possession of the fullness and the life that God desires us to have with him. Giants make cowards of us all. Giants make it difficult to trust. Medical reports, financial crises, insecurities, family conflicts, loneliness, depression, are all giants that can paralyze us with fear and keep us from being willing to be obedient. They can keep us from trusting God's promises and his word, and even his very heart. Giants cause us to doubt.

What is looming large in your life right now? What just looks too big and too overwhelming to overcome? How are those *giants* keeping you from the life God most wants for you these days? Listen to the words God gave the Israelites as they struggled with fear and take them for your own. Remember that he loves you. He will care for you. He will fight for you. He is trustworthy. So fear not!

Pray: Tell God your greatest fears and allow his word and his Spirit to give you strength and courage.

Closing Prayer: O Lord our God, help us to live our lives with the faith and courage necessary to live by love and not by fear. Forgive us when our seeing and our thinking get so distorted that we allow fear to control us and make us its slave. Seize our hearts with your perfect love and drive out all fear, no matter how big the *giants* might appear to be. In the name of Jesus. Amen.

Tuesday
Third Week of Lent

Come to Stillness: The Lord is in his holy temple; let all the earth be silent before him. (Habakkuk 2:20)

Opening Prayer: Forgive me, O God, when I demand that you dance to my tune, rather than me dancing to yours. Forgive me when I try to make you play by my rules, rather than me playing by yours. Forgive me when I try to determine the direction and agenda for my life, rather than me operating by yours. For when I do this it shows how far I still have to go — and to grow — in my relationship with you. I am still such a child in my faith; filled with childish ways and childish attitudes. Help me, O Jesus, to grow up fully into you. Be the One who always determines how I live my life. In your name and for your glory I pray. Amen.

Scripture: Luke 7:31-35

"To what then shall I compare the people of this generation, and what are they like? They are like children sitting in the marketplace and calling to one another,

> "'We played the flute for you, and you did not dance; we sang a dirge, and you did not weep.'

For John the Baptist has come eating no bread and drinking no wine, and you say, 'He has a demon.' The Son of Man has come eating and drinking, and you say, 'Look at him! A glutton and a drunkard, a friend of tax collectors and sinners!' Yet wisdom is justified by all her children." (ESV)

Journal: What are you demanding from God these days?

Where are you trying to make the rules?

Where are you trying to set the agenda and the direction?

What song are you playing that God is refusing to dance to?

Reflection: Let us never be mistaken about one thing: Jesus only comes to us on his terms, not on our own. We can never demand, control, or manipulate him — although we constantly try. Even though the incarnation proves that he is the God who *comes,* he does so on our *turf,* but only on his *terms.* He is the one in control and he will not give that up. We, therefore, cannot demand that God behave the way we want him to, or he just might not show up at all. For when we try to dictate the *how* and the *when* of his coming, we have stopped seeking him altogether. At that point we are no longer seeking God, we are seeking to become God.

Pray: Ask God to show you the areas of demandingness in your life.

Closing Prayer: Father, I abandon myself into Your hands; do with me what You will. Whatever You do I thank You. I am ready for all, I accept all. Let only Your will be done in me, as in all Your creatures, I ask no more than this, my Lord. Into Your hands I commend my soul; I offer it to You, O Lord, with all the love of my heart, for I love You, my God, and so need to give myself — to surrender myself into Your hands, without reserve and with total confidence, for You are my Father. ~Charles de Foucauld

Wednesday
Third Week of Lent

Come to Stillness: Guard your steps when you go to the house of God. To draw near to listen is better than to offer the sacrifice of fools, for they do not know that they are doing evil. Be not rash with your mouth, nor let your heart be hasty to utter a word before God, for God is in heaven and you are on earth. Therefore let your words be few. (Ecclesiastes 5:1-2, ESV)

Opening Prayer: Lord, give me the faith and courage to follow you, whatever it may cost, wherever it may lead. For the sake of Jesus. Amen.

Scripture: Luke 14:25-35

Now great crowds accompanied him, and he turned and said to them, "If anyone comes to me and does not hate his own father and mother and wife and children and brothers and sisters, yes, and even his own life, he cannot be my disciple. Whoever does not bear his own cross and come after me cannot be my disciple. For which of you, desiring to build a tower, does not first sit down and count the cost, whether he has enough to complete it? Otherwise, when he has laid a foundation and is not able to finish, all who see it begin to mock him, saying, 'This man began to build and was not able to finish.' Or what king, going out to encounter another king in war, will not sit down first and deliberate whether he is able with ten thousand to meet him who comes against him with twenty thousand? And if not, while the other is yet a great way off, he sends a delegation and asks for terms of peace. So therefore, any one of you who does not renounce all that he has cannot be my disciple.

"Salt is good, but if salt has lost its taste, how shall its saltiness be restored? It is of no use either for the soil or for the manure pile. It is thrown away. He who has ears to hear, let him hear." (ESV)

Journal: How do these words of Jesus strike you?

How do they disturb you?

How do they inspire you?

How do they challenge you?

How does your love for Jesus compare to your love for the other things in your life?

Reflection: This text seems like a pretty extreme statement doesn't it? It's very disturbing and disruptive, especially to our "have our cake and eat it too" mentality. Somehow we have tried to tame Jesus and his words. Somehow we have convinced ourselves that we can be "half in." But Jesus will not stand for that. He will not settle for less. He will not be tamed. He is wild and free. He is disruptive and disturbing. As John Powell once said. "He comforts the afflicted and afflicts the comfortable." You cannot "buy him" in small quantities; with him it is "all or nothing." Our problem is that we tend to want a limited quantity of him; "five dollars' worth," if you will. We want just enough to make us comfortable, but not so much that it disturbs our lives or disrupts our plans and agendas. But of course, Jesus will not operate by our rules. That's just the way he is. And as you read Luke 14:25-35 that becomes pretty clear.

Jesus doesn't just desire our love and allegiance, he demands it. In fact, if in comparison to our love for him we don't "hate" all else, we are not worthy of him. There is no room for negotiation, no room for debate. His love for us demands our full love and allegiance in return. If, indeed, we really want to follow him we can only do so with all of our being.

Pray: Have a conversation with Jesus today about the words of Luke 14:25-35. What do you want to say to him? What do you think he wants to say to you?

Closing Prayer: Take Lord, and receive all my liberty, my memory, my understanding, and my entire will, all that I have and possess. Thou hast given all to me. To Thee, O Lord, I return it. All is Thine, dispose of it wholly according to Thy will. Give me Thy love and thy grace, for this is sufficient for me. ~Ignatius Loyola

Thursday
Third Week of Lent

Come to Stillness: Spend a few minutes in silence, allowing your heart and soul to come to rest. This will create good space within you to hear God's voice.

Opening Prayer: Lord Jesus, when we see you as you really are, and see ourselves as we really are, we have no choice but to cry out like Simon Peter: "Depart from me for I am a sinful man, O Lord!" Because when we see your beauty and your greatness, we are completely captured and completely overwhelmed. All we want to do from that moment on is to become more and more like you, leaving all else behind to follow you — that is true discipleship. Amen.

Scripture: Luke 5:1-11

On one occasion, while the crowd was pressing in on him to hear the word of God, he was standing by the lake of Gennesaret, and he saw two boats by the lake, but the fishermen had gone out of them and were washing their nets. Getting into one of the boats, which was Simon's, he asked him to put out a little from the land. And he sat down and taught the people from the boat. And when he had finished speaking, he said to Simon, "Put out into the deep and let down your nets for a catch." And Simon answered, "Master, we toiled all night and took nothing! But at your word I will let down the nets." And when they had done this, they enclosed a large number of fish, and their nets were breaking. They signaled to their partners in the other boat to come and help them. And they came and filled both the boats, so that they began to sink. But when Simon Peter saw it, he fell down at Jesus' knees, saying, "Depart from me, for I am a sinful man, O Lord." For he and all who were with him were astonished at the catch of fish that they had taken, and so also were James and John, sons of Zebedee, who were partners with Simon. And Jesus said to Simon, "Do not be afraid; from now on you will be catching men." And when they had brought their boats to land, they left everything and followed him. (ESV)

Journal: What words in this passage speak most to your life right now?

Can you relate to Simon Peter? How?

What does it mean for you to *put out into the deep*?

What response arises in your soul as you watch the scene unfold?

What does it mean in your life to *catch men*?

Reflection: There are three movements in this story that give us a beautiful picture of what true discipleship is really all about. The first movement is an *invitation.* Jesus invites Simon Peter and his companions to *put out into the deep.* The Greek word used here is *bathos,* which can mean physical *depth,* but also means *profundity.* It is the same word that's used in Ephesians 3:18 to talk about the immeasurable love of God, and used again in 1 Corinthians 2:10 to talk about how the Spirit reveals to us the *deep* things of God. So Simon Peter and his friends are being invited not only to deeper waters, but also to deeper places in their lives with Jesus. For in the life of faith, God is always inviting us to deeper and deeper places with him. We can't simply stay in the shallows. We can't remain motionless and stagnant, we must move further and further into him. We must put out into the deep, the place where he sets the agenda and direction for our lives, the place where we can't reach the bottom, the place where we can't control or manage or determine our circumstances and outcomes, the place where we are in way over our heads. The deep is a place of total surrender, total trust, and total dependence. It is also the place of genuine encounter and transformation.

Which leads us to the second movement: *encounter.* In the deep we encounter Jesus in a life-changing way. We come face to face with who he really is and what he really wants both for us and from us. Once Peter obeys the call to *put out into the deep,* he makes a realization. His eyes are opened in a brand new way and it changes the way he sees everything: life, vocation, God, even himself. He begins to see how big and awesome and wonderful and beautiful Jesus really is. And, as a result, he is completely captured and completely overwhelmed by what he sees. His response tells it all, "*Depart from me for I am a sinful man, O Lord.*" In just a few short verses Peter has moved from seeing Jesus only as his *Master*, to now seeing Jesus as his *Lord*. For he realizes that anyone who could do something so amazing and miraculous must be the One to whom all things belong. And when Peter sees how big and powerful Jesus is, it immediately causes him to see how small and frail and broken he is himself. And as a result, a deep and wonderful humility is born within him, which we all know is some of the best possible soil for the life of the Spirit to grow. Because humility breaks us open. Humility totally destroys pride. Pride separates, but humility unites. Pride judges, but humility loves. Pride breeds condescension but humility breeds acceptance.

You see, God was doing a work in Simon Peter to get him ready for the next movement: *vocation.* Peter's encounter with Jesus redefines his life, his mission, and his purpose. No longer is Peter merely a fisherman; that is not his real vocation. His real vocation from now on is to catch men.

As it is with each of us. As a result of our encounter with Jesus, in the deep, our whole lives are *reoriented* according to his kingdom and his purposes. Thus, the question is no longer, "Where does Jesus fit into my life?" but, "Where do I fit in his kingdom and his purposes and what he is doing in the world?" Thus we, as these new disciples did, must pull our boats up on shore, whatever that might look like, leave everything behind, and follow him. That is true discipleship.

Pray: Have a conversation with Jesus today about *invitation, encounter,* and *vocation.*

Closing Prayer: Give us the courage to follow you, Lord Jesus, wherever you may lead and whatever it may cost. Make us true disciples. Amen.

Friday
Third Week of Lent

Come to Stillness: Be still and quiet before the Lord for the next few minutes. Make room within you for him to move and to act. Wait for him.

Opening Prayer: O Lord, our God, challenge us with your word this day. Let us listen to it with the ear of our hearts and wrestle with its truth. Let us submit to it that it may accomplish your purposes within us. Let us take care to heed it, even if it be a hard word, that we may always choose to follow you and thus have life. Amen.

Scripture: John 6:48-69

"I am the bread of life. Your fathers ate the manna in the wilderness, and they died. This is the bread that comes down from heaven, so that one may eat of it and not die. I am the living bread that came down from heaven. If anyone eats of this bread, he will live forever. And the bread that I will give for the life of the world is my flesh."

The Jews then disputed among themselves, saying, "How can this man give us his flesh to eat?" So Jesus said to them, "Truly, truly, I say to you, unless you eat the flesh of the Son of Man and drink his blood, you have no life in you. Whoever feeds on my flesh and drinks my blood has eternal life, and I will raise him up on the last day. For my flesh is true food, and my blood is true drink. Whoever feeds on my flesh and drinks my blood abides in me, and I in him. As the living Father sent me, and I live because of the Father, so whoever feeds on me, he also will live because of me. This is the bread that came down from heaven, not like the bread the fathers ate, and died. Whoever feeds on this bread will live forever." Jesus said these things in the synagogue, as he taught at Capernaum.

When many of his disciples heard it, they said, "This is a hard saying; who can listen to it?" But Jesus, knowing in himself that his disciples were grumbling about this, said to them, "Do you take offense at this? Then what if you were to see the Son of Man ascending to where he was before? It is the Spirit who gives life; the flesh is no help at all. The words that I have spoken to you are spirit and life. But there are some of you who do not believe." (For Jesus knew from the beginning who those were who did not believe, and who it was who would betray him.) And he said, "This is why I told you that no one can come to me unless it is granted him by the Father."

After this many of his disciples turned back and no longer walked with him. So Jesus said to the Twelve, "Do you want to go away as well?" Simon Peter answered him, "Lord, to whom shall we go? You have the words of eternal life, and we have believed, and have come to know, that you are the Holy One of God." (ESV)

Journal: What *hard word* has been given to you lately?

Are there any hard truths that Jesus has been trying to teach you? What are they?

What has your response been?

Reflection: *Difficulty* either seems to bring out the best or the worst in people. They seem to either rise to the occasion and meet difficulty with renewed strength, resolve, and determination, or they head for the hills. In our text the difficulty is in the form of a teaching; something that Jesus was saying that sounded pretty outlandish: *"Truly, truly, I say to you, unless you eat the flesh of the Son of Man and drink his blood, you have no life in you. Whoever feeds on my flesh and drinks my blood has eternal life, and I will raise him up on the last day. For my flesh is true food, and my blood is true drink. Whoever feeds on my flesh and drinks my blood abides in me, and I in him."*

Okay, I get it. I can see why they might think this is such a difficult teaching, especially if they were taking him literally rather than metaphorically. But even if they were able to see through the gory imagery to the essence of what Jesus was really trying to say, it is still a difficult teaching. Because we try to feed on so many things in this life besides God. We feed on success, we feed on attention, and we feed on affirmation. We feed on position, we feed on power, and we feed on prestige. We feed on popularity, we feed on possessions, and we feed on performance. You name it, we can feed on it.

That's what makes this teaching so difficult, because it is into the middle of this dysfunctional feeding frenzy that Jesus comes, telling us that: "You must feed on me to have any life in you." It is difficult to just stop, and turn from all of the people and the things and the places on which we feed, and turn only to Jesus. It is so hard, in fact, that we simply refuse to do it. The things of this life taste too good. The tricky part is that they taste great, but are less filling, to borrow a phrase from years gone by. And thus, we hear his call to feed on him and yet we still run off to our old familiar feeding places and gorge ourselves on food that cannot possibly satisfy the deepest longings our soul. For only his flesh is real food and only his blood is real drink — our souls can live on nothing else. This teaching was so difficult that it caused many to walk away from him that day. What response does it bring up in you? What will you do with this difficult teaching today? Will you turn to him? Will you feed on him? Or will you head for the hills?

Pray: Feed on him in your heart through prayer today.

Closing Prayer: Come, all you who are thirsty, come to the waters; and you who have no money, come, buy and eat! Come, buy wine and milk without money and without cost. Why spend money on what is not bread, and your labor on what does not satisfy? Listen, listen to me, and eat what is good, and you will delight in the richest of fare. Give ear and come to me; listen, that you may live. (Isaiah 55:1-3, NIV)

Saturday
Third Week of Lent

Come to Stillness: "Come to me, all you who are weary and burdened, and I will give you rest. Take my yoke upon you and learn from me, for I am gentle and humble in heart, and you will find rest for your souls. For my yoke is easy and my burden is light." (Matthew 11:28-30, NIV)

Opening Prayer: Lord, give us the courage and the perspective to count it all joy when we face hard times; knowing that through them you are going to do a great work in us. One that will make us more into the people you long for us to be. Amen.

Scripture: James 1:2-4

Count it all joy, my brothers, when you meet trials of various kinds, for you know that the testing of your faith produces steadfastness. And let steadfastness have its full effect, that you may be perfect and complete, lacking in nothing. (ESV)

Journal: What is your normal mindset when you go through trying times?

How is it possible to count it all joy?

How is God at work in your life right now in a hard, but good way?

Reflection: There is a distinct difference between joy and happiness. Happiness is mostly circumstantial; when suffering comes, happiness hits the road. But joy is much deeper, much more substantial. Joy is not dependent on conditions being favorable. In fact, joy is something that is able to endure the presence of pain and still abide. The word joy comes from the Greek word *chara* which means *a deep and sustaining gladness.* This gladness is able to see the bigger picture, and to trust in the sacred heart of the One who can bring beauty from ashes and victory from the jaws of defeat.

So when James tells us to *count it all joy when we face trials of many kinds,* he is not telling us we need to be happy about it. He is telling us to trust in the end result. He is telling us that beneath the sorrow, or the suffering, or the pain, is always a hand that is working in us to make us more and more into the people God desires us to be. This joy holds an unflinching trust in his unfailing love; trust that regardless of the circumstances, or the situation, he is always up to something good. Thanks be to God.

Pray: Have a conversation with God about all that is hard in your life right now. Will you trust him with it?

Closing Prayer: God of life and death, teach us to hold on to you in all circumstances, knowing that a deeper life is often the result of the trials we endure. Give us, O Lord, a prayerful heart that enables us to transcend our petty needs for security and significance, so that we may be free to rest in loving union with you, and trust that you are always a God who can bring beauty from ashes. Amen.

Fourth Sunday of Lent

Come to Stillness: "But oh! God is in his holy Temple! Quiet everyone—a holy silence. Listen!" (Habakkuk 2:20, *The Message*)

Opening Prayer: Lord God, I know my transgressions, and my sin is ever before me. Against you, you only, have I sinned and done what is evil in your sight, so that you may be justified in your words and blameless in your judgment. Behold, I was brought forth in iniquity, and in sin did my mother conceive me. Behold, you delight in truth in the inward being, and you teach me wisdom in the secret heart. Purge me with hyssop, and I shall be clean; wash me, and I shall be whiter than snow. Let me hear joy and gladness; let the bones that you have broken rejoice. Hide your face from my sins, and blot out all my iniquities. Create in me a clean heart, O God, and renew a right spirit within me. By the power, and the blood, of Jesus. Amen. (Psalm 51:3-10, NIV)

Scripture: Psalm 32:1-11

Blessed is the one whose transgression is forgiven,
    whose sin is covered.
Blessed is the man against whom the Lord counts no
    iniquity, and in whose spirit there is no deceit.
For when I kept silent, my bones wasted away
    through my groaning all day long.
For day and night your hand was heavy upon me;
    my strength was dried up as by the heat of summer.
I acknowledged my sin to you,
    and I did not cover my iniquity;

I said, "I will confess my transgressions to the Lord,"
and you forgave the iniquity of my sin.
Therefore let everyone who is godly
offer prayer to you at a time when you may be found;
surely in the rush of great waters, they shall not reach
him.
You are a hiding place for me;
you preserve me from trouble;
you surround me with shouts of deliverance. Selah
I will instruct you and teach you in the way you should
go; I will counsel you with my eye upon you.
Be not like a horse or a mule, without understanding,
which must be curbed with bit and bridle,
or it will not stay near you.
Many are the sorrows of the wicked,
but steadfast love surrounds the one who trusts in the
Lord.
Be glad in the Lord, and rejoice, O righteous,
and shout for joy, all you upright in heart! (ESV)

Journal: What has been your experience with the
practice of confession?

Are there things within you right now that are taking up space that God longs to occupy?

How might confession open up space within you for God to speak and act?

How might it unburden you inside?

What are the things you need to confess to God this day?

Reflection:
I want to unfold.
Nowhere do I want to remain folded,
because where I am folded, there I am a lie.
~Rainer Maria Rilke

A few years ago, at the end of a retreat I was leading, I got into a wonderful conversation with a dear friend about all that God was up to in our lives. Somewhere in the midst of that conversation he asked me a really good question: "Do you have any secrets?" The tone and the spirit of the question was not at all threatening or judgmental or harsh, but rather easy and free and filled with care. And I clearly remember being delighted with the answer that arose from deep within me. "You know," I said, "I really don't." And something wonderful was struck deep within me; not only by the answer, but also by the question. Because deep in my heart and soul I have an overwhelming desire to live openly, *unfolded*, before God and before the people in my life and world. This beautiful question was an invitation to do just that.

I've been thinking about confession a lot lately, and the role it plays in our life with God. So many times I have viewed confession as a shame-filled, guilt-laden process that no one in their right mind would want to perform on any kind of regular basis. But I'm beginning to think that I had it all wrong. Confession is not a practice that is meant to produce guilt and fear and shame, but one that holds within it the possibility of living truly and freely and wholly (or holy) before God and before one another. Confession is meant to produce life and space and freedom within me. It is meant to unburden me of all of the baggage I drag around on a regular basis. When I stand *open* before God and allow him to see all of me (which he already sees anyway), it does something beautiful deep within my soul. It opens up the possibility for intimacy and communication and growth (i.e., real relationship). It allows him to help me clean up my "inner room" of all of the junk and the mess and the clutter that fills the landscape of my soul and takes up room that God alone was meant to occupy. It *unfolds* me. Because living folded, closed, and hiding is not really life at all, but only a fear-filled lie. And we all know that: "There is no fear in love, but perfect love casts out fear. For fear has to do with punishment, and whoever fears has not been perfected in love." (1 John 4:18, ESV)

So I'm hoping that from this day forward I will begin to see confession in a new way; as an invitation and an opportunity rather than a duty and an obligation. An invitation from my loving Father to live before him (and in him) openly, freely, and *unfolded*. Thanks be to God!

Pray: Spend some time before God in confession today.

Closing Prayer: Make us holy, O Holy God, for you alone have the power to do such a thing. Left to our own will, our own strength, and our own devices we are without hope. We cannot make ourselves holy. Give us your holiness, Lord God. Wash us clean, O Lord, and give us the holiness of your son, our Savior, Jesus Christ. Make us holy, as he is holy. Amen.

Monday
Fourth Week of Lent

Come to Stillness: Spend a few minutes in silence, allowing your heart and mind to come to rest. This will help you pay attention to the movement of God within you and around you.

Opening Prayer: Lord Jesus, so many things and events and circumstances in this life cause me to lose my focus and take my eyes off of you. And when I do that, I sink. Lord Jesus, help me not to get distracted by the wind and the waves, but help me to keep my eyes firmly fixed on you. Amen.

Scripture: Matthew 14:22-33

Immediately after this, Jesus insisted that his disciples get back into the boat and cross to the other side of the lake, while he sent the people home. After sending them home, he went up into the hills by himself to pray. Night fell while he was there alone.

Meanwhile, the disciples were in trouble far away from land, for a strong wind had risen, and they were fighting heavy waves. About three o'clock in the morning Jesus came toward them, walking on the water. When the disciples saw him walking on the water, they were terrified. In their fear, they cried out, "It's a ghost!"

But Jesus spoke to them at once. "Don't be afraid," he said. "Take courage. I am here!"

Then Peter called to him, "Lord, if it's really you, tell me to come to you, walking on the water."

"Yes, come," Jesus said.

So Peter went over the side of the boat and walked on the water toward Jesus. But when he saw the strong wind and the waves, he was terrified and began to sink. "Save me, Lord!" he shouted.

Jesus immediately reached out and grabbed him. "You have so little faith," Jesus said. "Why did you doubt me?"

When they climbed back into the boat, the wind stopped. Then the disciples worshiped him. "You really are the Son of God!" they exclaimed. (NLT)

Journal: Where do you find yourself in this story? Why?

What *storms* in your life right now are causing you to take your eyes off of Jesus, and instead focus on the wind and the waves?

Reflection: *The soul must just leave itself in the hands of God, and do what he wills it to do, completely disregarding its own advantage and resigning itself as much as it possibly can to the will of God.* ~Teresa of Avila

It seems that when we are somehow able to keep our eyes focused on Jesus in this crazy life of faith, we are able to keep things in perspective for the most part. Yet, when we begin to look around us and focus instead on the wind and the waves, things can get pretty dicey really fast. We, like Simon Peter, begin to sink into the sea of our fear and our doubt and our anxiety and our despair.

It seems that as long as we spend our lives focused on our circumstances, we are in for a pretty wild ride. But if somehow we can—by God's grace and guidance—train ourselves to keep our eyes focused on Jesus, in all things and at all times, we can be certain that though the winds may blow and the waves may crash over us, Jesus always has us in his strong and loving hands. Thanks be to God!

Pray: Ask Jesus to calm the storms both around you and within you today.

Closing Prayer: Lord Jesus, though the winds may blow and the waves may crash over us, hold us safe in your strong and loving hands, this day and every day. Amen.

Tuesday
Fourth Week of Lent

Come to Stillness: Be still and know that I am God. (Psalm 46:10, ESV)

Opening Prayer: Lord, you are able. Help me to truly believe that. Amen.

Scripture: Matthew 9:27-31

And as Jesus passed on from there, two blind men followed him, crying aloud, "Have mercy on us, Son of David." When he entered the house, the blind men came to him, and Jesus said to them, "Do you believe that I am able to do this?" They said to him, "Yes, Lord." Then he touched their eyes, saying, "According to your faith be it done to you." And their eyes were opened. And Jesus sternly warned them, "See that no one knows about it." But they went away and spread his fame through all that district. (ESV)

Journal: "Do you believe that I am able to do this?"

What is *this* for you right now?

Reflection: What a great question: "Do you believe that I am able to do this?" It is a question that Jesus asked often in one form or another. It seems that faith and willingness were at least a help, if not a prerequisite, for healing to occur. I mean, how many times did Jesus utter the words: "Your faith has healed you," or ask the question, "Where is your faith?" How many times in the Gospels did he stop and marvel over and focus attention upon someone who had just done or said something that exhibited great faith? He even healed one man — the paralytic — because of the faith shown by his friends (Mark 2:5). Jesus obviously loved it when he looked into a heart and saw a hint (or an abundance) of belief. So faith really seems to matter to Jesus, or to at least be a significant factor in the equation.

Given that, I guess it is good for us to look deep into our hearts and answer the question as well. I guess it is good for us to stop, look into the loving eyes of our Savior, and hear him ask, "Do you really believe I am able to do this?" —whatever our *this* may be. Where in your life right now is that the burning question? Where in your life right now are you wishing and hoping and praying that Jesus might actually be able to do *this*? What is your answer to him today?

Pray: Have a conversation with Jesus today, answering the question, "Do you believe I am able to do this?"

Closing Prayer: Lord Jesus, help me *believe that you are able to do this*, whatever *this* may be in my life at the moment. Have mercy on me. Amen.

Wednesday
Fourth Week of Lent

Come to Stillness: Spend a few minutes just being with God — no demands, no agenda, just sitting quietly in his presence.

Opening Prayer: O God, anchor our souls in the hope that your promises are all true. Help us find peace and comfort in the faithfulness of your character, in spite of our circumstances. Hold us fast when the storms of life are blowing us around so much that we are afraid that at any moment we might crash upon the rocks of life. Be our strength and our shield, O God, our shelter from the storm. Through Jesus we pray. Amen.

Scripture: Hebrews 6:13-20

When God made his promise to Abraham, since there was no one greater for him to swear by, he swore by himself, saying, "I will surely bless you and give you many descendants." And so after waiting patiently, Abraham received what was promised.

People swear by someone greater than themselves, and the oath confirms what is said and puts an end to all argument. Because God wanted to make the unchanging nature of his purpose very clear to the heirs of what was promised, he confirmed it with an oath. God did this so that, by two unchangeable things in which it is impossible for God to lie, we who have fled to take hold of the hope set before us may be greatly encouraged. We have this hope as an anchor for the soul, firm and secure. It enters the inner sanctuary behind the curtain, where our forerunner, Jesus, has entered on our behalf.

He has become a high priest forever, in the order of Melchizedek. (NIV)

Journal: What is the state of your soul these days?

How are you being tossed about?

What is anchoring your soul?

Reflection: *Anchor* – a person or thing that can be relied on for support, stability, or security; a mainstay. The Greek word is *agkyra*, which is used four times in the entire New Testament; once here in Hebrew 6:19, and the other three times in Acts 27. The three instances in the book of Acts all refer to a literal anchor on a ship; that which provides safety, stability, and security. The anchor is the thing that keeps you from crashing into the rocks, or keeps you from getting tossed about by the sea, or keeps you docked securely in the harbor. It doesn't offer to change the circumstances, but offers to help you in the midst of them.

Here in Hebrews the word is used metaphorically to describe the effect God desires for hope to have on our souls. Hope (in God's promises) is meant to be an anchor *for our souls*, to keep us safe and secure in the midst of the storms and chaos of life. The promise is not that the seas will be smooth, or that the storms will stop, or even that everything will turn out alright. The promise is that even if the circumstances never improve, his promises will be an anchor *for our souls*.

The only thing about an anchor is that in order for it to work, it has to be used. An anchor does no good sitting inside the ship, it must be tossed into the sea. Nor does hope in God's promises do us any good if they are never tossed into the raging sea of our fear and doubt and anxiety. Once we rely on, and trust in, his promises — which remind us of his heart and his character — as our soul's anchor, then, and only then, will we find that "the rope holds."

Pray: Pray that God would be your anchor. Allow him to hold you securely in his love today.

Closing Prayer: Disturb us, Lord, when we are too pleased with ourselves, when our dreams have come true because we dreamed too little, when we arrived safely because we sailed too close to the shore.

Disturb us, Lord, when with the abundance of things we possess we have lost our thirst for the waters of life; having fallen in love with life, we have ceased to dream of eternity and in our efforts to build a new earth, we have allowed our vision of the new heaven to dim.

Disturb us, Lord, to dare more boldly, to venture on wilder seas where storms will show your mastery; where losing sight of land, we shall find the stars. We ask you to push back the horizons of our hopes; and to push back the future in strength, courage, hope, and love. This we ask in the name of our Captain, who is Jesus Christ. ~Sir Francis Drake

Thursday
Fourth Week of Lent

Come to Stillness: Take a few minutes and be silent before the Lord, so that you might hear what he wants to say to you today.

Opening Prayer: Lord Jesus, help us to be like you; willing to lay aside our rights and privileges, willing to empty ourselves and humble ourselves, willing to become *of no reputation,* for your sake and your kingdom and your glory. Amen.

Scripture: Philippians 2:1-13

Therefore if there is any encouragement in Christ, if there is any consolation of love, if there is any fellowship of the Spirit, if any affection and compassion, make my joy complete by being of the same mind, maintaining the same love, united in spirit, intent on one purpose. Do nothing from selfishness or empty conceit, but with humility of mind regard one another as more important than yourselves; do not *merely* look out for your own personal interests, but also for the interests of others. Have this attitude in yourselves which was also in Christ Jesus, who, although He existed in the form of God, did not regard equality with God a thing to be grasped, but emptied Himself, taking the form of a bond-servant, *and* being made in the likeness of men. Being found in appearance as a man, He humbled Himself by becoming obedient to the point of death, even death on a cross. For this reason also, God highly exalted Him, and bestowed on Him the name which is above every name, so that at the name of Jesus every knee will bow, of those who are in heaven and on earth and under the earth, and that every tongue will confess that Jesus Christ is Lord, to the glory of God the Father.

So then, my beloved, just as you have always obeyed, not as in my presence only, but now much more in my absence, work out your salvation with fear and trembling; for it is God who is at work in you, both to will and to work for *His* good pleasure. (NASB)

Journal: Where is God doing a work of humility within you? How?

How is this making you more like Jesus?

Will you embrace this process the way Jesus did? How?

Reflection: God has been teaching me a lot about humility lately; some through prayer and scripture, and some through hard experience. He is teaching me about the great value of being unnoticed, unseen, and unnecessary. He has actually been teaching me about these things for years, but finally, I think (and hope), I am beginning to embrace what he is trying to do in me. Madeleine L'Engle once wrote: "*When we are self-conscious, we cannot be wholly aware; we must throw ourselves out first.*" It seems that this *throwing ourselves out* is what the work of humility is all about, so that we might be fully aware of God, and what he desires, and what he is up to within and around us.

Humility is such a good and beautiful — and terrible — thing. It creates such open, receptive soil in our souls. It opens our ears, and our hearts, to God's voice because it keeps us from being so full of our own. Humility brings about freedom and wholeness because it releases us from the burden of constantly having something to prove. It empties us of *self* and creates space for God to move and to act by preparing our souls to receive whatever he might desire to plant in us. It is a *dying* that makes way for a *living*. It is an *emptying* that makes space for a *filling*. It is an *absence* that makes us aware of a *presence*. It is a *sorrow* that brings about a *joy*. It is a *letting go* that leads to a *taking hold*. And I have a suspicion that this work of humility God is doing within me is not so much a season as it is a destination — calling me to a new way of being.

Eugene Peterson said it this way: "*When God became human in Jesus, he showed us how to be complete human beings before him. We do it the way Jesus did it, by becoming absolutely needy and dependent on the Father. Only when we stand emptied, stand impoverished before God can we receive what only empty hands can receive. This is the poverty of spirit in which Jesus blesses us (Matt. 5:3)."*

Pray: Pray that God would give you the same attitude as that of his Son, Jesus. Pray for a work of genuine humility to take place deep within you.

Closing Prayer: Lord Jesus, let humility do its work in me: *emptying* me of self, *opening* my ears to your voice, *softening* my heart to those around me, and *allowing* me to be, and to love, more like you each day. Amen.

Friday
Fourth Week of Lent

Come to Stillness: For God alone my soul waits in silence; from him comes my salvation. He alone is my rock and my salvation, my fortress; I shall not be greatly shaken. (Psalm 62:1-2, ESV)

Opening Prayer: O creative God, who dreamt me into being before the foundations of the world. Give me the strength, the courage, and the conviction to become all that you desire for me to be. Mold me and form and shape me, that I might be conformed more and more to your image. In the name of Jesus. Amen. (*Pieces II* by Jim Branch)

Scripture: Luke 6:43-45

For no good tree bears bad fruit, nor again does a bad tree bear good fruit, for each tree is known by its own fruit. For figs are not gathered from thornbushes, nor are grapes picked from a bramble bush. The good person out of the good treasure of his heart produces good, and the evil person out of his evil treasure produces evil, for out of the abundance of the heart his mouth speaks. (ESV)

Journal: How does a fig tree grow figs?

What kind of tree are you these days?

What is growing on your branches?

What kind of tree do you long to be?

How will you be that?

Reflection: How does a fig tree grow figs? No, it's not a trick question. But it's not rocket science either. A fig tree grows figs by being what it was created to be. When it is planted in fertile soil, and tended with care and attention, and watered by the spring rains, it will grow figs. That's just who and what it is. If it tries to grow apples, or peaches — or anything other than figs for that matter — it's in for a rough go of it. It kind of makes you wonder why we ever try to be anything other than who we are.

The converse is also true. If you want to know what kind of a tree you have before you, just look at the fruit it produces and it will tell you everything you need to know. Figs are not produced by thorn bushes and grapes are not grown on bramble bushes. Thus, a good tree does not produce bad fruit, and vice versa. The kind of fruit that is growing on the vines and branches of our lives will tell us the truth about what is going on inside. So, as you look at the branches of your life these days, what do they tell you?

Pray: Ask God to help you be who and what he created you to be. Listen to him today, and allow him to tell you just who (and what) that is.

Closing Prayer: Help me, O God, to surrender my life completely to your control and command. Give it both a plan and pattern that constantly reminds me of your presence and consistently makes me more responsive to your will. For the sake of Jesus, your Son. Amen. (*Pieces II* by Jim Branch)

Saturday
Fourth Week of Lent

Come to Stillness: Sit quietly before God for a few minutes and let your mind and heart come to rest. This will allow you to be fully present to whatever God might want to do in you today.

Opening Prayer: Lord Jesus, help me to live my life this day as a *son* rather than a *slave*. Do not let fear turn me into something I no longer am; help me instead to know that I am a beloved child of the Father. Amen.

Scripture: Romans 8:14-17

For all who are led by the Spirit of God are sons of God. For you did not receive the spirit of slavery to fall back into fear, but you have received the Spirit of adoption as sons, by whom we cry, "Abba! Father!" The Spirit himself bears witness with our spirit that we are children of God, and if children, then heirs — heirs of God and fellow heirs with Christ, provided we suffer with him in order that we may also be glorified with him. (ESV)

Journal: Do you feel mostly like a slave to fear or like a son/daughter of God today?

How are you living as a slave to fear today?

How does being a child of God offer you freedom from that life of fear?

Will you accept it?

Reflection: I live as a slave when I start living in fear of what might happen. I live as a slave when I live my life afraid that I do not have what it takes, that I don't measure up, that I am not enough, that I am of no value. Then I become a slave not only to fear, but also a slave to circumstance, a slave to comparison, a slave to competition, and a slave to affirmation, achievement, and applause. That is when I must cling to the truth that I am not a slave, but a son. In fact, I am your beloved son. You delight in me. When I truly believe this, then, and only then, will I ever be free. Free to live as you live and free to love as you love.

Pray: Listen to the Voice that calls you a beloved.

Closing Prayer: Lord Jesus, help me to love like you love today. By the power of your Spirit within me, remind me that I am your child, and rid my heart of all that is not love. Amen.

Fifth Sunday in Lent

Come to Stillness: Sit silently for a few minutes before God in prayer. Let go of all your plans, demands and agendas, and just surrender yourself to his care and to his presence.

Opening Prayer:
Dear God,
   Please untie the knots that are in my mind my heart and my life. Remove the have *nots*, the can *nots*, and the do *nots* I have in my mind. Erase the will *nots*, may *nots*, the might *nots* that may find a home in my heart. Release me from the would *nots* could *nots* and should *nots* that obstruct my life. And most of all, remove from my mind my heart and my life, the am *nots* that I have allowed to hold me back especially the thought that I am not good enough. Amen. (Author unknown)

Scripture: John 13:31-38

   When he was gone, Jesus said, "Now the Son of Man is glorified and God is glorified in him. If God is glorified in him, God will glorify the Son in himself, and will glorify him at once.
   "My children, I will be with you only a little longer. You will look for me, and just as I told the Jews, so I tell you now: Where I am going, you cannot come.
   "A new command I give you: Love one another. As I have loved you, so you must love one another. By this everyone will know that you are my disciples, if you love one another."
   Simon Peter asked him, "Lord, where are you going?"

Jesus replied, "Where I am going, you cannot follow now, but you will follow later."

Peter asked, "Lord, why can't I follow you now? I will lay down my life for you."

Then Jesus answered, "Will you really lay down your life for me? Very truly I tell you, before the rooster crows, you will disown me three times!" (NIV)

Journal: Will you really lay down your life for him?

Reflection: *"Will you really lay down your life for me?"* What a question! In fact, it might actually be THE question as we get closer to the beginning of Holy Week. Are we really willing to go all the way to the cross with Jesus? Are we really willing to take up our cross, whatever it may be, and follow him? Are we really willing to die with him, that we might be raised with him?

Peter said he was willing, but when it came right down to it, was he really? When times got tough and the cost of following Jesus was his very life, would he really be willing to die? We obviously know the rest of the story, so we know how this ended. For Simon Peter it ended in a denial, but what about us?

Imagine Jesus turning to you and asking you the very same question: *"Will you really lay down your life for me? Will you? This very moment, and the next, and the next?"* What is your answer? And what does that even look like? In the weeks ahead we are going to see what that looks like; Jesus is going to give us a great example. Obviously he was willing to lay down his life for us; now are we willing to do the same?

Pray: Answer that question today in prayer.

Closing Prayer: O God, who by your One and only Son has overcome death and opened to us the gate of everlasting life; grant, we pray, that those who have been redeemed by his passion may rejoice in his resurrection, through the same Christ our Lord. Amen. ~Gelasian Sacramentary

Monday
Fifth Week of Lent

Come to Stillness: Allow your soul to come to rest before God. Give all of your thoughts, fears, anxieties, and insecurities to him. Ask him to quiet your heart, that you might be able to hear his voice.

Opening Prayer: Lord Jesus, deliver us from those things in our lives from which we just can't break free. We simply do not have the power. But you do! Give us your divine power to destroy the strongholds in our lives, for apart from you we have no hope of victory. Amen.

Scripture: 2 Corinthians 10:1-6

By the humility and gentleness of Christ, I appeal to you – I, Paul, who am "timid" when face to face with you, but "bold" toward you when away! I beg you that when I come I may not have to be as bold as I expect to be toward some people who think that we live by the standards of this world. For though we live in the world, we do not wage war as the world does. The weapons we fight with are not the weapons of the world. On the contrary, they have divine power to demolish strongholds. We demolish arguments and every pretension that sets itself up against the knowledge of God, and we take captive every thought to make it obedient to Christ. And we will be ready to punish every act of disobedience, once your obedience is complete. (NIV)

Journal: What destructive patterns have created strongholds in your life?

Do you really want freedom from them?

Do you believe that Jesus offers you divine power to destroy those strongholds?

Will you let him fight for you?

Will you surrender these areas completely to him and let him destroy them?

Tell him that...

Reflection: Freedom never comes cheaply. It always costs something, and most often something significant. Battles are waged over freedom. Why would we expect the life of the Spirit to be any different? If we truly want to live lives of freedom it will require some bloodshed — most likely our own. We are going to have to muster all of our courage and go down to the places within us where the most heroic battles are fought. We are going to have to face some opponents that are not pretty to look at, mostly because *"they* are *us."*

We are going to have to face our own inner reality and be willing to fight our own inner ugliness with all that is within us. We are going to have to allow the Spirit to destroy things in us that run so deep that their excision will feel like our death. And in many ways it will be, for until those things die completely they will not stop breathing their foul-smelling stench within us.

We are going to have to allow the Spirit of God, with the weapons of the Spirit, to wage a full on attack of the sinful patterns and habits that run to our core, and put them to death once and for all. Only then will we ever have any hope that these strongholds will be destroyed. And only then will we be truly free.

Pray: Present the areas of bondage in your life to Jesus this day in prayer. Surrender them to him. Ask for his strength and *divine power to demolish* these strongholds and give you the freedom you were created for.

Closing Prayer: Lord Jesus, I surrender all of my life to you. Give me strength where I am weak, give me hope where I am discouraged, and give me freedom where I am bound. By your divine power. Amen.

Tuesday
Fifth Week of Lent

Come to Stillness: A wise man once said that our souls are like a pond: when the waters are disturbed and agitated it is impossible to see what is underneath. Only when we allow the waters of our souls to become still and calm will there ever be any real hope of seeing and hearing God in the core of our being. Take a few minutes and allow the waters of your soul to become still and calm.

Opening Prayer: O Christ Jesus, when all is darkness and we feel our weakness and helplessness, give us the sense of your presence, your love, and your strength. Help us to have perfect trust in your protecting love and strengthening power, so that nothing may frighten or worry us, for, living close to you, we shall see your hand, your purpose, your will through all things. ~St. Ignatius

Scripture: Matthew 14:23-32

Immediately Jesus made the disciples get into the boat and go on ahead of him to the other side, while he dismissed the crowd. After he had dismissed them, he went up on a mountainside by himself to pray. Later that night, he was there alone, and the boat was already a considerable distance from land, buffeted by the waves because the wind was against it.

Shortly before dawn Jesus went out to them, walking on the lake. When the disciples saw him walking on the lake, they were terrified. "It's a ghost," they said, and cried out in fear.

But Jesus immediately said to them: "Take courage! It is I. Don't be afraid."

"Lord, if it's you," Peter replied, "tell me to come to you on the water."

"Come," he said.

Then Peter got down out of the boat, walked on the water and came toward Jesus. But when he saw the wind, he was afraid and, beginning to sink, cried out, "Lord, save me!"

Immediately Jesus reached out his hand and caught him. "You of little faith," he said, "why did you doubt?" And when they climbed into the boat, the wind died down. Then those who were in the boat worshiped him, saying, "Truly you are the Son of God." (NIV)

Journal: Where is Jesus calling you to *step out of your boat* these days?

What does that look like?

Where is he calling you to deeper places with him?

Where is he calling you to deeper trust?

Reflection: If nothing else you have to admire Peter's willingness. I mean, at least he desired to step out of the boat and move toward Jesus — and dared to do so. It was not an easy step, to say the least. The step into deep waters never is. It requires a lot. Jesus was asking Peter to leave the security of the boat and his friends and his old life and ways, and to join him in a totally new and totally unfamiliar place. A place of total surrender and total abandon. That's what life with God is all about. We can't avoid it or deny it.

And when Jesus invites us to that place with him it always requires us to *step out* of our comfortable and controlled lives (and ways) and *step into* a life that is completely determined and ordered by him. It is a place where complete trust is necessary and where real life is experienced. Peter took Jesus up on his invitation, but most of us never get that far. Most of us hear the call of Jesus to a radical trust and somehow determine that this level of commitment is for someone else. Most of us hear his invitation to a deeper life with him and allow the wind and the waves to scare us off, long before we ever consider stepping out onto the raging sea.

Peter's willingness meant that he was able to experience something that he never could have experienced inside the boat. But first he had to step out. Which is often the case with each of us. So often we are simply unwilling — be it from fear, or preoccupation, or comfort, or control and agenda — to step out onto the sea with Jesus, where we must totally trust his care and his control. The sea is so wild and deep and untamed. It is a place where we cannot touch bottom, where we cannot control things, where we cannot manage life on our own terms. The sea is a place where we have no idea, or control over, what will happen when we finally set feet upon its waters. Therefore, it is a place of total vulnerability, total surrender, and total trust. Peter was willing to go there. He stepped out. He took nothing with him. He completely let go of everything else but this burning desire to be with Jesus, wherever Jesus might lead, whatever Jesus might ask.

The call of Jesus is like that for us all. Are we willing to take that step, whatever that step may look like? Are we willing to join him? If we really want to be his, there is no other choice.

Pray: Ask God what it looks like to *step out of your boat*. Talk with him about your willingness to do so. Give him your fears and ask him to give you the courage to follow him onto the wild and raging sea.

Closing Prayer: Lord Jesus, give me a willingness to respond to your invitation to step out of my boat, whatever that may mean, and to follow you as I step out onto the raging sea. Amen.

Wednesday
Fifth Week of Lent

Come to Stillness: Only when we are open and empty will we ever be truly able to receive whatever it is that God is longing to give us of himself. When our hands, and thus our hearts, are full of agendas and plans, expectations and demands, then we are indeed too full of *ourselves* to ever be able to see or to notice — much less receive — the gift of God's peace and His presence.

Somewhere a surrender must take place, a giving up and a giving over of all that so often fills our hearts and our souls. A dying, an emptying of self in order to make room for God's Spirit and *God's grace* to do its work in us. Take a few minutes and try to empty yourself of all but God, in order that he might fill you with himself.

Opening Prayer: O Lord, help us to not lose heart when times get hard, but instead help us to cling tightly to you. By your Spirit guard us, protect us, and renew us. Help us to realize that these light and momentary struggles are achieving for us an eternal weight of glory that is beyond all comparison. Help us, O Lord, when things look bleak, to always keep our eyes firmly fixed on you — the unseen God — rather than on the visible circumstances around us. In the name and power of Jesus we pray. Amen.

Scripture: 2 Corinthians 4:16-18

Therefore we do not lose heart. Though outwardly we are wasting away, yet inwardly we are being renewed day by day. For our light and momentary troubles are achieving for us an eternal glory that far outweighs them all. So we fix our eyes not on what is seen, but on what is unseen, since what is seen is temporary, but what is unseen is eternal. (NIV)

Journal: In what ways are you most tempted to lose heart these days?

What is the cause of that?

How do you feel like your "outer self" is wasting away?

How is your "inner self" being renewed day by day?

What does it specifically mean for you, this week, to *fix your eyes on the unseen* rather than what is seen?

Reflection: It sounds kind of bizarre really, this *fixing our eyes on what is unseen.* I mean, what does that even look like? And how do we really do that?

It is so easy to fix our eyes on what is seen, what is right there in front of us. I guess Paul knew the truth of the old saying that *looks can be deceiving.* Because, in this life of faith, it is not what we can see that is *most* real, it is what we cannot see, which is so counter-intuitive. But what we can see is often merely a façade, a covering that conceals something much deeper and truer to be seen if we will just look beneath the surface. If we will just look into the heart of things. If we will just look into the heart of God. If we will turn our eyes from the physical to the spiritual. For it is not our outer selves that matter the most, it is our *inner selves.* It is not the part of us that is *wasting away* that counts the most, but the part that is *being renewed day by day.* That is to be our focal point.

If we fix our eyes on our *light and momentary struggles,* they will seem neither light nor momentary. In fact, they will feel overwhelming, paralyzing, and debilitating. They will actually gain momentum and power over us the more we *fix our eyes* on them.

But if we, instead, *fix our eyes* on what is unseen, on that which is being accomplished by God within us and among us, something else happens altogether—hope is born, courage is grown, character is enlarged, and perseverance is cultivated. Fixing our eyes on what is unseen creates and nurtures a longing deep within us for home—our true home. And thus, even though outwardly we might still be wasting away, inwardly we are being renewed day by day.

Pray: Ask God to focus your eyes on what is unseen today. What do you see?

Closing Prayer: Lord, when I am tempted to look around me, and let what I can see determine how I live my life, turn my eyes toward you and allow me to see the depths of your love and affection. Let the things that are unseen be the things that determine who I am and what I do. Let my hope be built on things that are eternal. In the name of Jesus I pray. Amen.

Thursday
Fifth Week of Lent

Come to Stillness: Be still and quiet for a few minutes before your God. Know that he is near and that he desires your undivided attention. Give that to him right now.

Opening Prayer: Lord Jesus, give us the grace and the strength to trust your heart, even when we can't see your hand. Amen.

Scripture: Luke 7:11-17

Soon afterward, Jesus went to a town called Nain, and his disciples and a large crowd went along with him. As he approached the town gate, a dead person was being carried out—the only son of his mother, and she was a widow. And a large crowd from the town was with her. When the Lord saw her, his heart went out to her and he said, "Don't cry."

Then he went up and touched the coffin, and those carrying it stood still. He said, "Young man, I say to you, get up!" The dead man sat up and began to talk, and Jesus gave him back to his mother.

They were all filled with awe and praised God. "A great prophet has appeared among us," they said. "God has come to help his people." This news about Jesus spread throughout Judea and the surrounding country. (NIV)

Journal: How are you like the widow of Nain?

Where is God in the midst of the pain in your life?

How do you think he feels about it?

Reflection: Where is God when we are in pain? It is an age-old question. One that, depending on how we answer it, can significantly impact our view of, and our relationship with, God. Because when we are in pain our tendency is to think that God either does not care, or that he is not good. Either he does not care enough to do anything about our suffering, or he can't do anything about it. Or, maybe even worse, he won't do anything about it. All of which leaves us either angry and frustrated, or anxious and insecure.

Then along comes Jesus, the one who was sent to reveal to us the heart of the Father. Jesus, since he is God in the flesh, shows us exactly how God feels about our pain. And not only that, he also shows us how God longs to redeem that pain, in his own time and in his own way.

On this occasion Jesus crosses paths with a woman who has just lost her only son, and that after she had already lost her husband. Can you imagine the grief and the sadness and the pain? Maybe you can. Maybe you have been there. Maybe you are there. Life has dealt her two crushing blows back-to-back, and she is left reeling. "Where in the world is God?" she must be asking in the midst of the chaos, "Doesn't he even care?"

Enter Jesus. And when Jesus sees her, immediately his *heart goes out to her* (NIV). He is *heartbroken* (The Message). His *heart overflows with compassion* (NLT). He is moved with love and compassion for her from the very depths of his being. That is how God feels about her pain. That is how God feels about your pain. He is brokenhearted. Her broken life is not at all the way he intended it to be. But, even still, in the midst of her grief, God is able to redeem her pain.

Jesus stops the procession, approaches the coffin, places his hand on it, and calls the young man back to life. The young man sits up and begins to speak. Then Jesus *gives the young man back to his mother.* God redeems her pain. God brings life out of death, just the way he always does. Tears turn to laughter, sadness to joy, mourning to dancing. And that is the way it will be for your pain as well. Maybe not today, but someday. Someday your pain will be redeemed. Someday your sorrow will be turned to joy. Someday Jesus will tenderly touch your face and wipe away every tear from your eyes. And sorrow and sadness will be no more.

And *they were all filled with awe and praised God* (NIV), the Scriptures tell us. *"God has come to help his people,"* they said. In fact, *he has turned his face towards his people* (JBP). God is not distant. He is not disinterested. He is not uncaring. He is not far off. He is right here, right in the midst of our pain.

Why is there so much pain and suffering in the world? The only honest answer to that question is that I have absolutely no idea. How does God feel about that pain and suffering, and where is he in the midst of it? The answer to those two questions are a little more clear, all because of Jesus. God is heartbroken over our pain. And he is right in the middle of it. That's why he came to earth in the first place: to both share our suffering and to bear our suffering, that one day it might all be redeemed.

Prayer: Tell God how you are feeling about your pain today, and then listen for his response.

Closing Prayer: Thank you, Lord Jesus, that you have promised that one day you will turn my mourning into dancing. O how I long for that day! Amen.

Friday
Fifth Week of Lent

Come to Stillness: Stop for a moment and allow yourself to become still and quiet inside. This might take a while, but it is necessary if you want to really spend time with God today. Otherwise, you will be too full of yourself to really be with him.

Opening Prayer: O Lord Jesus, how we hate the wilderness! But it is such a necessary part of the spiritual journey. Even you had to spend time there, because God was somehow doing a mysterious work in you in the midst of it. So help us to know that the wilderness is a place of struggle, but also a place of deep encounter. It is a place of presence, not a place of absence. For in the wilderness you get our attention in a way that you couldn't get it any other place.

Scripture: Isaiah 43:16-19

See, I am doing a new thing! Now it springs up; do you not perceive it? I am making a way in the wilderness and streams in the wasteland. (NIV)

Journal: Where are you on your spiritual journey these days?

In what ways are you in the wilderness?

What do you think God is up to in the midst of it?

What *new thing* is he doing in you these days?

Reading for Reflection: It is so easy at times to get completely consumed with the *wilderness* we find ourselves in the midst of, that we are unable to see the God who is *making a way* for us in the midst of it, much less the *new thing* he is trying to do both in and through us as a result. I guess that's because we have a tendency to get so consumed with *where we are* in our own lives and journeys, so caught up in our own smaller stories, that we cannot see the larger story of God and where he is leading us and what he is doing in our lives and in our world.

Being in the *wilderness* is a necessary part of the process. The saints called it *purgation*. It is the part of the journey where we empty ourselves — or God empties us — of whatever we might be full of other than God. It is the part of the journey where we make room within us to *receive* whatever *new thing* God might want to do in us. For if we are too full — of guilt, or shame, or fear, or anxiety, or insecurity, or even ambition — then there is no room for God to work. *Purgation* makes space for *illumination* (the second part of the ancient dance), which then brings us to the possibility of *union*, the thing God desires most, both for us and from us.

The problem is that if we end up in the *wilderness* for a substantial amount of time, we begin to believe that that's all there is. We forget that there is more to the story. We forget that this season is *making a way* for something good and beautiful. We forget that *purgation* is simply one part of a much larger dance. In fact, we can become so consumed with whatever *wilderness* we find ourselves in, that we really can't see anything else.

Therefore, it is essential to remind ourselves of, and engage in, the larger story. When we focus on the larger story, of God and his work in our lives and our world, then it gives us perspective and hope. Therefore, we must not get caught up — or consumed, or stuck — in the smaller story, but continually push ourselves to look beyond it. Because God is always about a larger story, and all of our smaller stories only make sense in light of his story.

Pray: Talk with God about your journey and where you find yourself these days. Ask him to show you the *new thing* he is doing within you. And ask him how your story fits in to the larger story of what he is doing in the world.

Closing Prayer: Lord, enfold me in the depths of your heart; and there hold me, refine, purge, and set me on fire, raise me aloft, until my own self knows utter annihilation. ~Pierre Teilhard de Chardin

Saturday
Fifth Week of Lent

Come to Stillness: Be still, O my soul, that I might hear the voice of the one who calls me beloved.

Opening Prayer: O Lord my God, teach my heart this day where and how to see you, and where and how to find you. ~St. Anselm

Scripture: John 10:22-42

Then came the Festival of Dedication at Jerusalem. It was winter, and Jesus was in the temple courts walking in Solomon's Colonnade. The Jews who were there gathered around him, saying, "How long will you keep us in suspense? If you are the Messiah, tell us plainly."

Jesus answered, "I did tell you, but you do not believe. The works I do in my Father's name testify about me, but you do not believe because you are not my sheep. My sheep listen to my voice; I know them, and they follow me. I give them eternal life, and they shall never perish; no one will snatch them out of my hand. My Father, who has given them to me, is greater than all; no one can snatch them out of my Father's hand. I and the Father are one."

Again his Jewish opponents picked up stones to stone him, but Jesus said to them, "I have shown you many good works from the Father. For which of these do you stone me?"

"We are not stoning you for any good work," they replied, "but for blasphemy, because you, a mere man, claim to be God."

Jesus answered them, "Is it not written in your Law, 'I have said you are "gods"'? If he called them 'gods,' to whom the word of God came – and Scripture cannot be set aside – what about the one whom the Father set apart as his very own and sent into the world? Why then do you accuse me of blasphemy because I said, 'I am God's Son'? Do not believe me unless I do the works of my Father. But if I do them, even though you do not believe me, believe the works, that you may know and understand that the Father is in me, and I in the Father." Again they tried to seize him, but he escaped their grasp.

Then Jesus went back across the Jordan to the place where John had been baptizing in the early days. There he stayed, and many people came to him. They said, "Though John never performed a sign, all that John said about this man was true." And in that place many believed in Jesus. (NIV)

Journal: The Words of Jesus both comfort and disrupt. Which one do they do in you today? Why?

What words are words of consolation to your soul today? How?

What words are words of disruption today? Why?

How do you try to seize Jesus and attempt to make him behave the way you want him to?

Reflection:

Again they tried to seize him,
but he escaped their grasp. (john 10:39)

Jesus
Lord Jesus
We can never seize you
Any better than *they* could
So I wonder why
We keep on trying

You are always
Too big for us
And too small
You are always
Escaping our grasp
Thanks be to God

Pray: Talk with God today about your deepest struggle with belief.

Closing Prayer: Lord Jesus, you are wild and untamed. You are too much for us. Forgive us when we try to box you in and make you a manageable size. Forgive us when we try to take hold of you and domesticate you. Forgive us when we make demands of you and try to manipulate you. Be wild and free in our lives, and allow us to be the same in you. Amen.

Palm Sunday

Come to Stillness: Sit with Jesus for a few minutes and simply keep company with him — no words, no requests, and no agendas. Just be with him and allow him to calm your heart and still your soul.

Opening Prayer: Lord Jesus, today we join you on your ride into Jerusalem. Today we hear the shouts of *Hosanna!* Today we lay our coats and our palm leaves on the road, but we both know that once we get to Jerusalem everything will change. For we know why you are going there. You are going there to die. And you invite us to do the same.

Give us the courage to ride with you this day and to walk with you this week. Give us the strength to stay awake with you in the garden, to not abandon you in the melee, and to follow you closely all the way to Golgotha. It is Holy Week, O Lord, so may we walk with you this week in full awareness of all that will take place — and why. Amen.

Scripture: Mark 11:1-11

As they approached Jerusalem and came to Bethphage and Bethany at the Mount of Olives, Jesus sent two of his disciples, saying to them, "Go to the village ahead of you, and just as you enter it, you will find a colt tied there, which no one has ever ridden. Untie it and bring it here. If anyone asks you, 'Why are you doing this?' say, 'The Lord needs it and will send it back here shortly.'"

They went and found a colt outside in the street, tied at a doorway. As they untied it, some people standing there asked, "What are you doing, untying that colt?" They answered as Jesus had told them to, and the people let them go. When they brought the colt to Jesus and threw their cloaks over it, he sat on it. Many people spread their cloaks on the road, while others spread branches they had cut in the fields. Those who went ahead and those who followed shouted,

"Hosanna!"

"Blessed is he who comes in the name of the Lord!"

"Blessed is the coming kingdom of our father David!"

"Hosanna in the highest heaven!"

Jesus entered Jerusalem and went into the temple courts. He looked around at everything, but since it was already late, he went out to Bethany with the Twelve. (NIV)

Journal: What is going on within you as we begin Holy Week?

Are you ready for this journey to the cross?

What will that mean for you this year?

Reflection:

> come
> ride with me
> beckons jesus
> come
> to jerusalem
> come
> and weep
> over a city
> gone astray
> come
> and die with me
> that you might
> be raised
> to new life
> (*Pieces II* by Jim Branch)

Pray: Have a conversation with Jesus as you ride together into Jerusalem. What do you want to say to him? What do you think he wants to say to you?

Closing Prayer: Lord Jesus, what was in your heart as you rode into Jerusalem? What was on your mind? What were your thoughts? What were your prayers?

As we begin this Holy Week, may we be good companions to you on this journey of love. Thank you for the depths to which you were willing to go in order to show us how deeply we are loved. Amen.

Monday of Holy Week

Come to Stillness: Spend a few minutes in silence before the Lord. Be fully present to him. This will open you up to receive whatever it is that he has to give you today.

Opening Prayer: O God of life, in times and in seasons where I tend to be focused only on what is dead and dying, either within me or around me, help me to know that, in your economy, death always leads to life. Give me faith to believe that the season of *unless a kernel of wheat falls to the ground and dies* is always followed by the season of *if it dies it produces many seeds.* Thank you for that truth. Amen.

Scripture: John 12:23-28

Jesus replied, "The hour has come for the Son of Man to be glorified. Very truly I tell you, unless a kernel of wheat falls to the ground and dies, it remains only a single seed. But if it dies, it produces many seeds. Anyone who loves their life will lose it, while anyone who hates their life in this world will keep it for eternal life. Whoever serves me must follow me; and where I am, my servant also will be. My Father will honor the one who serves me.

"Now my soul is troubled, and what shall I say? 'Father, save me from this hour'? No, it was for this very reason I came to this hour. Father, glorify your name!"

Then a voice came from heaven, "I have glorified it, and will glorify it again." (NIV)

Journal: Where in your life are you sensing that something must die in order for many seeds to be produced?

What is it?

What is your "kernel?"

What are the "many seeds"?

Where in your life have you seen evidence of life coming out of death?

Reflection:

a longing
for genuine transformation
will always lead us
to death's door
again and again

what a crazy design
a kernel of wheat must die
and fall to the ground
in order for it to become
many seeds
life from death
paschal mystery

the old must be
out of the way
in order to
make space
for the new
to be born
within us

one cannot truly begin
without the other ending
release comes
before receive

after all
it is impossible
to receive the new
when our hands are still
so full of the old

that's why death
is such a necessary part
of the process
because
without death
there can be
no resurrection

and resurrection
is really the point
being raised, that is,
not raising ourselves

being raised
by the giver of life
breathing his breath
into our deadness
and bringing us
to life once again
in a new form
that is not new
at all
to him

Pray: Talk with God about what must die in you in order to be raised to new life.

Closing Prayer: Thank you, O God, that spring always follows winter, that Easter always follows Good Friday, and that resurrection always follows death!!! Thank you that when a kernel of wheat falls to the ground and dies, it always produces many seeds. Thank you, O God, that death does not have the final word, but life does. We praise you O God of life!!!

Tuesday of Holy Week

Come to Stillness: In the garden of Gethsemane Jesus asked his closest friends to stay awake and keep him company. Unfortunately, they were not up to the task. Sit with Jesus for a few minutes, just enjoying his company, and allowing him to enjoy yours. This will ready your heart and make it open and receptive to whatever he might have to say.

Opening Prayer: Lord Jesus, help us to keep watch and pray with you in this time. Keep our souls awake and attentive to whatever you might want to say. Amen.

Scripture: Matthew 26:36-46

Then Jesus went with his disciples to a place called Gethsemane, and he said to them, "Sit here while I go over there and pray." He took Peter and the two sons of Zebedee along with him, and he began to be sorrowful and troubled. Then he said to them, "My soul is overwhelmed with sorrow to the point of death. Stay here and keep watch with me."

Going a little farther, he fell with his face to the ground and prayed, "My Father, if it is possible, may this cup be taken from me. Yet not as I will, but as you will."

Then he returned to his disciples and found them sleeping. "Couldn't you men keep watch with me for one hour?" he asked Peter. "Watch and pray so that you will not fall into temptation. The spirit is willing, but the flesh is weak."

He went away a second time and prayed, "My Father, if it is not possible for this cup to be taken away unless I drink it, may your will be done."

When he came back, he again found them sleeping, because their eyes were heavy. So he left them and went away once more and prayed the third time, saying the same thing.

Then he returned to the disciples and said to them, "Are you still sleeping and resting? Look, the hour has come, and the Son of Man is delivered into the hands of sinners. Rise! Let us go! Here comes my betrayer!" (NIV)

Journal: What would it have been like to be with Jesus in the garden of Gethsemane?

How would you have felt if you were one of the disciples?

What would you want to say to him?

What do you want to say to him now?

What is your response to the willingness of Jesus to accept the cross?

Reflection: His soul was *overwhelmed with sorrow to the point of death*. His sweat was *like drops of blood falling to the ground* (Luke 22:44). He was in total agony over what was about to unfold, fully knowing everything that was ahead of him. So he begged his closest friends to *"Stay here and keep watch with me."* Surely they would be able to stand with him for just one hour. But, in his time of greatest need, his dearest friends let him down. They fell asleep! Humanly speaking, he was all alone.

So he turned to his Father and cried out, *"My Father, if it is possible, may this cup be taken from me. Yet not as I will, but as you will."* Is that not amazing? Somehow, in spite of all that was stacked against him, Jesus was still willing. Willing to do whatever the Father asked. Willing to drink every drop of the *cup* that was before him. Willing to pay the heavy price that we rightly deserved. Willing to die for those that could not stay awake and watch with him for even one hour.

So, as we stand squarely in the middle of Holy Week, we have the opportunity once again to *watch with him*, whatever that may look like. We have the opportunity to sit with him and watch the agony, to hear the cries, to see the resolve, to be overwhelmed with gratitude over his willingness, to be captured by his love. Will we? Or will we fall asleep?

Pray: Watch and pray with Jesus in the garden today. Thank him for his willingness. Grieve the high cost of your sin. Be captured by his love.

Closing Prayer: Lord Jesus, help us to stay awake with you. Help us to watch with you as this Holy Week unfolds. Help us to celebrate your willingness. Help us to be overwhelmed and overcome by your sorrow. Help us to be captured by your love. Amen.

Wednesday of Holy Week

Come to Stillness: Take a few minutes and just breathe. Stop thinking about all you've got to do today, and all that causes you unrest, and simply breathe. Let go of your worries and your cares. Give them to God and allow him to take care of them for the next hour or so. Breathe in his life-giving Spirit, and breathe out the cares of this world.

Opening Prayer: Lord Jesus, you gave us your body and your blood, so that we might remember your love and your sacrifice until the day we are reunited with you in your Father's kingdom. Feed us now, during this time, with the bread of your body. And give us drink by the covenant of your blood, that our souls may adore you, delight in you, and come alive in you this day. Amen.

Scripture: Matthew 26:14-30

Then one of the twelve, whose name was Judas Iscariot, went to the chief priests and said, "What will you give me if I deliver him over to you?" And they paid him thirty pieces of silver. And from that moment he sought an opportunity to betray him.

Now on the first day of Unleavened Bread the disciples came to Jesus, saying, "Where will you have us prepare for you to eat the Passover?" He said, "Go into the city to a certain man and say to him, 'The Teacher says, My time is at hand. I will keep the Passover at your house with my disciples.'" And the disciples did as Jesus had directed them, and they prepared the Passover.

When it was evening, he reclined at table with the twelve. And as they were eating, he said, "Truly, I say to you, one of you will betray me." And they were very sorrowful and began to say to him one after another, "Is it I, Lord?" He answered, "He who has dipped his hand in the dish with me will betray me. The Son of Man goes as it is written of him, but woe to that man by whom the Son of Man is betrayed! It would have been better for that man if he had not been born." Judas, who would betray him, answered, "Is it I, Rabbi?" He said to him, "You have said so."

Now as they were eating, Jesus took bread, and after blessing it broke it and gave it to the disciples, and said, "Take, eat; this is my body." And he took a cup, and when he had given thanks he gave it to them, saying, "Drink of it, all of you, for this is my blood of the covenant, which is poured out for many for the forgiveness of sins. I tell you I will not drink again of this fruit of the vine until that day when I drink it new with you in my Father's kingdom."

And when they had sung a hymn, they went out to the Mount of Olives. (ESV)

Journal: What would it have been like to have been in the upper room?

What would your response have been?

How would you have felt when Jesus handed you the bread and the wine?

What does the invitation to this holy meal do within you?

What does it fill you with?

Reflection: *"Feed on him in your hearts by faith with thanksgiving,"* say the words of the ancient prayer, and what rich and wonderful words they are! They are words that invite us into a holy mystery. They are words that invite us to find our soul's deepest nourishment and sustenance in the body and blood of Jesus.

The sacraments act as doorways, or entry points into the type of union that God most deeply desires with each of us. They are physical signs that point to deep spiritual realities. All of which gives us an inside view of God's heart and his deep desire for relationship with us.

John, the disciple whom Jesus loved, knew this well. He was the one who had his head lying on the chest of Jesus as this evening meal unfolded (John 13:23-25). He was the one who could hear the very heartbeat of God. Therefore, he is our model for what this holy meal is all about; it is God's invitation to know his deep affection, to feast on his extravagant love, and to feed our hearts and our souls on his holy presence.

Judas Iscariot, by contrast, was also a part of this holy meal. In fact, he was offered the exact same invitation to *take and eat*. Except, it would appear, that his chief desire was to feed on something else altogether; be it money, or be it power, or be it some horrible combination of the two. Apparently, somewhere along the line, his appetite for the things of this world had grown far bigger than his appetite for God. Thus, Judas became a type of warning for all who come after. A warning that each of us must examine ourselves before we eat the bread and drink the cup, lest we eat and drink judgment on ourselves.

So in this meal Jesus invites each of us to partake of his body and blood. He comes to each of us and says: "Take, eat; this is my body. It is for you." And we are left with a choice. Will we feed on him and his love and his sacrifice, or will we turn to other people and places, to our old familiar feeding grounds, to gorge ourselves on food that cannot justify, nor satisfy. For, as he told us, *his flesh is real food and his blood is real drink*, and our souls can live on nothing else. What will we do with this invitation today? Will we sit down at his table and join him? Or will we hurry off into the night to feed on the things of this world rather than the things of God?

Pray: Sit at the table with Jesus and have a conversation with him. What do you want to say to him? What do you want to ask him? What does he want to say to you?

Closing Prayer: Lord Jesus, thank you for offering us yourself as food for our souls. May we gladly accept that invitation. Allow us to feed on you each day, for nothing else will satisfy our deepest longings. Amen.

Maundy Thursday

Come to Stillness: Spend a few minutes sitting silently before God, allowing your heart and mind to come to rest. This will help you to be attentive to his voice and alert to his presence as you spend time with him.

Opening Prayer: Lord Jesus, help us to understand that unless you wash us we can have no part with you. So wash us clean, O Savior, that we might be clean indeed. And that we might follow the example of service and sacrifice that you have given us to follow. Amen.

Scripture: John 13:1-15

It was just before the Passover Festival. Jesus knew that the hour had come for him to leave this world and go to the Father. Having loved his own who were in the world, he loved them to the end.

The evening meal was in progress, and the devil had already prompted Judas, the son of Simon Iscariot, to betray Jesus. Jesus knew that the Father had put all things under his power, and that he had come from God and was returning to God; so he got up from the meal, took off his outer clothing, and wrapped a towel around his waist. After that, he poured water into a basin and began to wash his disciples' feet, drying them with the towel that was wrapped around him.

He came to Simon Peter, who said to him, "Lord, are you going to wash my feet?"

Jesus replied, "You do not realize now what I am doing, but later you will understand."

"No," said Peter, "you shall never wash my feet."

Jesus answered, "Unless I wash you, you have no part with me."

"Then, Lord," Simon Peter replied, "not just my feet but my hands and my head as well!"

Jesus answered, "Those who have had a bath need only to wash their feet; their whole body is clean. And you are clean, though not every one of you." For he knew who was going to betray him, and that was why he said not everyone was clean.

When he had finished washing their feet, he put on his clothes and returned to his place. "Do you understand what I have done for you?" he asked them. "You call me 'Teacher' and 'Lord,' and rightly so, for that is what I am. Now that I, your Lord and Teacher, have washed your feet, you also should wash one another's feet. I have set you an example that you should do as I have done for you." (NIV)

Journal: What do you think it would have been like to have Jesus wash your feet?

What would your reaction have been?

What is your reaction to hearing that he has "given us an example that we should do as he has done to us"?

How will you follow the example of Jesus?

Reflection: *Unless I wash you, you have no part with me.* *(John 13:8)* One of my good friends always used to say, "You can come to Jesus with dirty feet, but you can't stay that way." And I wonder if that was not exactly what Jesus was trying to communicate to Simon Peter on this particular night. *Come to me. O come, you who are dirty and messy and broken. Come to me, all of you who are screwed up and fouled up and lost. Come to me, all who are anxious and fearful and insecure. Come to me, all who are filled with guilt and doubt and shame. Come to me, you whose feet – and hearts and lives – are covered with filth, and I will make you new. For you cannot wash yourselves, I must wash you. I can make the foulest heart clean. I can turn your mess into maturity. I can make the most broken life whole. Just come to me. But if you come to me, you must realize that you cannot stay the way you are, because everything that I touch, I transform. It is just the nature of who I am. I make things back into what they were intended to be. So come to me, for unless I wash you, you can have no part with me. What do you say?*

Pray: Imagine yourself sitting in the upper room. Watch closely as Jesus makes his way around the room, washing each of the disciples' feet. Notice the expression on his face. Notice the tenderness of his touch. Now he comes to you. He kneels at your feet, and takes them gently in his strong hands. How do you feel? What do you want to say to him? What does it look like to do this same thing to others? Whose feet is he asking you to wash?

Closing Prayer: Wash me, Blessed Jesus, wash me clean; for I am in desperate need. Wash my dirty feet, that I might offer others the same. Amen.

Good Friday

Come to Stillness: Quiet your heart and sit for a few minutes in silence before God today, allowing him to calm your mind and give your soul peace. This will help you to be fully present to all you will see and hear during this time.

Opening Prayer: By your cross, O Lord, you show the extravagance of your love for us. Love that knows no limits, no boundaries. Love that pours down upon us from every wound of your beloved Son. More love than we could ever ask for or imagine. When we are tempted to doubt the depths of your heart for us, let our eyes immediately look to Jesus crucified, and may all doubt be taken away. In His name. Amen.

Scripture: Matthew 26:47-27:56

The words were barely out of his mouth when Judas (the one from the Twelve) showed up, and with him a gang from the high priests and religious leaders brandishing swords and clubs. The betrayer had worked out a sign with them: "The one I kiss, that's the one — seize him." He went straight to Jesus, greeted him, "How are you, Rabbi?" and kissed him.

Jesus said, "Friend, why this charade?"

Then they came on him — grabbed him and roughed him up. One of those with Jesus pulled his sword and, taking a swing at the Chief Priest's servant, cut off his ear.

Jesus said, "Put your sword back where it belongs. All who use swords are destroyed by swords. Don't you realize that I am able right now to call to my Father, and twelve companies—more, if I want them—of fighting angels would be here, battle-ready? But if I did that, how would the Scriptures come true that say this is the way it has to be?"

Then Jesus addressed the mob: "What is this—coming out after me with swords and clubs as if I were a dangerous criminal? Day after day I have been sitting in the Temple teaching, and you never so much as lifted a hand against me. You've done it this way to confirm and fulfill the prophetic writings."

Then all the disciples cut and ran.

The gang that had seized Jesus led him before Caiaphas the Chief Priest, where the religion scholars and leaders had assembled. Peter followed at a safe distance until they got to the Chief Priest's courtyard. Then he slipped in and mingled with the servants, watching to see how things would turn out.

The high priests, conspiring with the Jewish Council, tried to cook up charges against Jesus in order to sentence him to death. But even though many stepped up, making up one false accusation after another, nothing was believable.

Finally two men came forward with this: "He said, 'I can tear down this Temple of God and after three days rebuild it.'"

The Chief Priest stood up and said, "What do you have to say to the accusation?"

Jesus kept silent.

Then the Chief Priest said, "I command you by the authority of the living God to say if you are the Messiah, the Son of God."

Jesus was curt: "You yourself said it. And that's not all. Soon you'll see it for yourself:

The Son of Man seated at the right hand of the

Mighty One,
Arriving on the clouds of heaven."
At that, the Chief Priest lost his temper, ripping his robes, yelling, "He blasphemed! Why do we need witnesses to accuse him? You all heard him blaspheme! Are you going to stand for such blasphemy?"

They all said, "Death! That seals his death sentence." Then they were spitting in his face and banging him around. They jeered as they slapped him: "Prophesy, Messiah: Who hit you that time?"

All this time, Peter was sitting out in the courtyard. One servant girl came up to him and said, "You were with Jesus the Galilean."

In front of everybody there, he denied it. "I don't know what you're talking about."

As he moved over toward the gate, someone else said to the people there, "This man was with Jesus the Nazarene."

Again he denied it, salting his denial with an oath: "I swear, I never laid eyes on the man."

Shortly after that, some bystanders approached Peter. "You've got to be one of them. Your accent gives you away."

Then he got really nervous and swore. "I don't know the man!"

Just then a rooster crowed. Peter remembered what Jesus had said: "Before the rooster crows, you will deny me three times." He went out and cried and cried and cried.

In the first light of dawn, all the high priests and religious leaders met and put the finishing touches on their plot to kill Jesus. Then they tied him up and paraded him to Pilate, the governor.

Judas, the one who betrayed him, realized that Jesus was doomed. Overcome with remorse, he gave back the thirty silver coins to the high priests, saying, "I've sinned. I've betrayed an innocent man."

They said, "What do we care? That's *your* problem!" Judas threw the silver coins into the Temple and left. Then he went out and hung himself.

The high priests picked up the silver pieces, but then didn't know what to do with them. "It wouldn't be right to give this — a payment for murder! — as an offering in the Temple." They decided to get rid of it by buying the "Potter's Field" and use it as a burial place for the homeless. That's how the field got called "Murder Meadow," a name that has stuck to this day. Then Jeremiah's words became history:

> They took the thirty silver pieces,
> The price of the one priced by some sons of Israel,
> And they purchased the potter's field.

And so they unwittingly followed the divine instructions to the letter.

Jesus was placed before the governor, who questioned him: "Are you the 'King of the Jews'?" Jesus said, "If you say so."

But when the accusations rained down hot and heavy from the high priests and religious leaders, he said nothing. Pilate asked him, "Do you hear that long list of accusations? Aren't you going to say something?" Jesus kept silence — not a word from his mouth. The governor was impressed, really impressed.

It was an old custom during the Feast for the governor to pardon a single prisoner named by the crowd. At the time, they had the infamous Jesus Barabbas in prison. With the crowd before him, Pilate said, "Which prisoner do you want me to pardon: Jesus

Barabbas, or Jesus the so-called Christ?" He knew it was through sheer spite that they had turned Jesus over to him.

While court was still in session, Pilate's wife sent him a message: "Don't get mixed up in judging this noble man. I've just been through a long and troubled night because of a dream about him."

Meanwhile, the high priests and religious leaders had talked the crowd into asking for the pardon of Barabbas and the execution of Jesus.

The governor asked, "Which of the two do you want me to pardon?"

They said, "Barabbas!"

"Then what do I do with Jesus, the so-called Christ?"

They all shouted, "Nail him to a cross!"

He objected, "But for what crime?"

But they yelled all the louder, "Nail him to a cross!"

When Pilate saw that he was getting nowhere and that a riot was imminent, he took a basin of water and washed his hands in full sight of the crowd, saying, "I'm washing my hands of responsibility for this man's death. From now on, it's in your hands. You're judge and jury."

The crowd answered, "We'll take the blame, we and our children after us."

Then he pardoned Barabbas. But he had Jesus whipped, and then handed over for crucifixion.

The soldiers assigned to the governor took Jesus into the governor's palace and got the entire brigade together for some fun. They stripped him and dressed him in a red toga. They plaited a crown from branches of a thornbush and set it on his head. They put a stick in his right hand for a scepter. Then they knelt before him in mocking reverence: "Bravo, King of the Jews!" they said. "Bravo!" Then they spit on him and hit him on the head with the stick. When they had had their fun, they took off the toga and put his own clothes back on him. Then they proceeded out to the crucifixion.

Along the way they came on a man from Cyrene named Simon and made him carry Jesus' cross. Arriving at Golgotha, the place they call "Skull Hill," they offered him a mild painkiller (a mixture of wine and myrrh), but when he tasted it he wouldn't drink it.

After they had finished nailing him to the cross and were waiting for him to die, they whiled away the time by throwing dice for his clothes. Above his head they had posted the criminal charge against him: THIS IS JESUS, THE KING OF THE JEWS. Along with him, they also crucified two criminals, one to his right, the other to his left. People passing along the road jeered, shaking their heads in mock lament: "You bragged that you could tear down the Temple and then rebuild it in three days—so show us your stuff! Save yourself! If you're really God's Son, come down from that cross!"

The high priests, along with the religion scholars and leaders, were right there mixing it up with the rest of them, having a great time poking fun at him: "He saved others—he can't save himself! King of Israel, is he? Then let him get down from that cross. We'll *all* become believers then! He was so sure of God—well, let him rescue his 'Son' now—if he wants him! He did claim to be God's Son, didn't he?" Even the two criminals crucified next to him joined in the mockery.

From noon to three, the whole earth was dark. Around midafternoon Jesus groaned out of the depths, crying loudly, "*Eli, Eli, lema sabachthani?*" which means, "My God, my God, why have you abandoned me?"

Some bystanders who heard him said, "He's calling for Elijah." One of them ran and got a sponge soaked in sour wine and lifted it on a stick so he could drink. The others joked, "Don't be in such a hurry. Let's see if Elijah comes and saves him."

But Jesus, again crying out loudly, breathed his last. At that moment, the Temple curtain was ripped in two, top to bottom. There was an earthquake, and rocks were split in pieces. What's more, tombs were opened up, and many bodies of believers asleep in their graves were raised. (After Jesus' resurrection, they left the tombs, entered the holy city, and appeared to many.)

The captain of the guard and those with him, when they saw the earthquake and everything else that was happening, were scared to death. They said, "This has to be the Son of God!"

There were also quite a few women watching from a distance, women who had followed Jesus from Galilee in order to serve him. Among them were Mary Magdalene, Mary the mother of James and Joseph, and the mother of the Zebedee brothers. (The Message)

Journal: What is your response to the cross?

What do you want say to the crucified Jesus today?

Reflection: I stand at the cross today with Jesus, looking into his eyes, wondering how in the world he could love me this much. I am totally overwhelmed. I am overwhelmed by his pain, his loneliness, his brokenness, and his sacrifice. I am overwhelmed, and overcome, by the power of his Great Affection. And I am overwhelmed by the enormous cost of my sin.

I am also overwhelmed by the suffering and the sorrow, the sadness and the grief, that surrounds him. What must this day have been like for his mother? For his brothers? For his friends? For all those who loved him so? The sadness and the grief, even in the midst of holding onto the hope of eternal life, must have been immense. Having recently stood in the midst of those who have lost one who was dearly loved, I can only imagine the pain. Having lost a child of my own long ago, it is not hard to remember the anguish and the agony of that loss, even though I know that someday we will be reunited.

On this Good Friday, what are we to do with all of this? It seems that there are two options. On the one hand we can endure and embrace it. Or, on the other, we can allow it to eat us alive from the inside out. Caryll Houselander once wrote: "*No one can escape it; everyone must somehow either make friends with suffering or be broken by it. No one can come close to another, let alone love him, without coming close to his suffering. Christ did far more, he wed himself to our suffering, he made death his bride, and in the consummation of his love, he gave her his life.*" So somehow, in embracing our pain, we not only join hands with the God who embraced and redeemed our own suffering, but we also hold on to the possibility that this pain will, someday, help us to be joined to him (and to each other) in a wonderfully intimate way that is beyond our imagination..

But I think the grief and sadness of Good Friday, ultimately, has something to teach us about the heart of God; a God we tend to blame and grow embittered against whenever suffering barges into our well-ordered, once-peaceful lives. As M. Robert Mulholland Jr. writes: "*God's most profound self-revelation is seen in the cross. We usually think of the cross as something God 'did' to 'solve' the sin problem that alienates us from God. But in reality, the cross reveals who God is, not what God did as an action separate from God's nature.*" The cross, and Good Friday, is not meant merely to show us what God did, but to show us who he is. He is not one who stands far off from us, orchestrating the tragedies in our lives. Nor is he one who stands idly by, refusing to use his power for our benefit, just to test us to see it we've *got what it takes.* He is a good, good Father. One who enters into the chaos with us. One who willingly watches his own Son be put to death by the very people he came to save; in order that they might one day come to know the joy and delight they were made to live in. He is a Father, even as the events of Good Friday unfold, whose heart breaks in grief and in agony over the necessity of the whole endeavor. So much so that he blackens the sun, he causes the earth to shake, and he tears his heavenly robes — the curtain of the temple — in grief as his Son Jesus cries out and breathes his last.

Where is God on Good Friday? He is grieving right along with us . . . . waiting for Sunday to come. Thanks be to God!

Pray: Fix your eyes on the crucified Jesus today. Tell him what is going on in your heart.

Closing Prayer: O most holy and loving God, we are awestruck when we fix our eyes upon the cross of Christ. We are awestruck at the depths of your love. We are awestruck at the extent of your holiness. We are awestruck at the completeness of your character. The cross, O Lord, is not just something you did, but it shows us who you are. Thank you. Amen.

Holy Saturday

Come to Stillness: Spend a few minutes in silence allowing your soul and spirit to come to stillness before God. This will prepare your heart to receive whatever he may have for you today.

Opening Prayer: O Lord, our God, so much of this life is lived *in between*: between the now and the not yet, between arriving and departing, between birth and death and rebirth, between growing up and growing old, between questions and answers. Help us not to live only for some distant day when the *in between* will be no more, but help us to step into the mystery of that sacred space here and now — knowing that it will be a place of genuine change and true transformation. (*The Blue Book* by Jim Branch)

Scripture: Luke 23:50-56

Now there was a man named Joseph, a member of the Council, a good and upright man, who had not consented to their decision and action. He came from the Judean town of Arimathea, and he himself was waiting for the kingdom of God. Going to Pilate, he asked for Jesus' body. Then he took it down, wrapped it in linen cloth and placed it in a tomb cut in the rock, one in which no one had yet been laid. It was Preparation Day, and the Sabbath was about to begin.

The women who had come with Jesus from Galilee followed Joseph and saw the tomb and how his body was laid in it. Then they went home and prepared spices and perfumes. But they rested on the Sabbath in obedience to the commandment. (NIV)

Journal: What does it feel like to stand between death and resurrection?

How is that place descriptive of your life these days?

Where are you living between death and resurrection?

Reflection:

But they rested on the Sabbath
in obedience to the commandment.
~Luke 23:56

it is not yet time
to go to the tomb
this is the in between time

grief has given way
to rest for now
and all we can do
is wait
and hope

death is the day gone by
but life is still yet to arrive
no angels
no visitations
no resurrection
no, not yet
it will come soon enough
but not today

today is holy saturday
today all we can do
is wait
and rest
and hope

Pray: Talk some with God today about that *in between*
space. What does that look like for you? Ask him what
he is up to in the midst of it.

Closing Prayer: Lord Jesus, help me to trust you as I stand between something dying within me and something being raised to life again. It is a scary and unsure place to be. Give me, this day, a trust in your care and a confidence in your love that will help me stand firm in this time of *the now and the not yet*. Amen.

Easter Sunday

Come to Stillness: Spend a few minutes in silence allowing your soul and spirit to come to stillness before God. Stillness allows your heart to be attentive and responsive to whatever God might have to say to you today.

Opening Prayer: Lord Jesus, I'm so glad Easter is finally here. During this season train my eyes and my heart to see you, O Risen Christ, in ways and in places that I don't normally see you. Thanks be to God that you are alive! *He is risen! He is risen indeed! Hallelujah!*

Scripture: Mark 16:1-8

When the Sabbath was over, Mary Magdalene, Mary the mother of James, and Salome bought spices so that they might go to anoint Jesus' body. Very early on the first day of the week, just after sunrise, they were on their way to the tomb and they asked each other, "Who will roll the stone away from the entrance of the tomb?"

But when they looked up, they saw that the stone, which was very large, had been rolled away. ⁵ As they entered the tomb, they saw a young man dressed in a white robe sitting on the right side, and they were alarmed.

"Don't be alarmed," he said. "You are looking for Jesus the Nazarene, who was crucified. He has risen! He is not here. See the place where they laid him. But go, tell his disciples and Peter, 'He is going ahead of you into Galilee. There you will see him, just as he told you.'"

Trembling and bewildered, the women went out and fled from the tomb. They said nothing to anyone, because they were afraid. (NIV)

Journal: Put yourself in the scene. Walk with Mary to the empty tomb. What do the words *"He has risen!"* mean to you today?

What is raised to life in you?

Reflection: What was it like in that dark tomb, Jesus? What exactly happened when light suddenly broke into the darkness and brought you to life once again? Did the mouth of God come down from heaven and breathe the breath of life into your lifeless body? Or did he reach down with his life-giving hands and brush the death from you as one would wipe sleep from the eyes of a child? Or was it like a Father tenderly bending down over his sleeping child to plant a gentle kiss upon his forehead? Perhaps it was more like an earthquake; a sudden jolt of power and life that hit you like a lightning bolt from on high, raising you suddenly to life once more.

And were there any words uttered in that silent grave? Words that you had the privilege of hearing, but that we will never know about because they were words meant only for your ears: a*rise, my love,* or *wake up sleepy head* or *My Child, I've missed you so much!*

And what was it like when the grave clothes were removed? And who exactly did that? Was it the angels who were present the next morning; sent by the Father to unbind his beloved Son? And why exactly did they fold them and stack them so neatly? I'll bet they were smiling from ear to ear.

And O what a reunion there must have been, the Three-in-One becoming Three and becoming One once more! What was that like? What was it like when you and the Father, and the Spirit, were reunited? What were the looks on your faces? What was going on in your hearts? What a dance that must've been! A dance we are now invited to join. O the joy, joy unspeakable.

Let our imaginations run wild on this Easter day, as we dream about, and celebrate, the day our beloved Jesus was raised to life again!

Pray: Sit in the presence of the risen Jesus today. What do you want to say to him? What do you think he wants to say to you? Tell him what you long to see *risen* in your life.

Closing Prayer: O God, our heavenly Father, today we join with your people throughout the world to celebrate the resurrection of your Divine Son, Jesus. We celebrate the fact that his victory over death has opened the way to eternal life. By the power of his resurrection and by your Spirit within us, O God, raise us up and renew our lives as well. We ask this through our Lord Jesus Christ, your Son, who lives and reigns with you and the Holy Spirit, one God, now and forevermore. Amen.

Monday
First Week of Easter

Come to Stillness: Spend a few minutes in silence allowing your soul and spirit to come to stillness before God. It is very important not to skip this part, it will prepare your heart to receive whatever he may have for you today.

Opening Prayer: Lord Jesus, you are risen indeed. Raise what is dead and dying in me to new life this day. Amen.

Scripture: John 20:1-18

Early on the first day of the week, while it was still dark, Mary Magdalene went to the tomb and saw that the stone had been removed from the entrance. So she came running to Simon Peter and the other disciple, the one Jesus loved, and said, "They have taken the Lord out of the tomb, and we don't know where they have put him!"

So Peter and the other disciple started for the tomb. Both were running, but the other disciple outran Peter and reached the tomb first. He bent over and looked in at the strips of linen lying there but did not go in. Then Simon Peter came along behind him and went straight into the tomb. He saw the strips of linen lying there, as well as the cloth that had been wrapped around Jesus' head. The cloth was still lying in its place, separate from the linen. Finally the other disciple, who had reached the tomb first, also went inside. He saw and believed. (They still did not understand from Scripture that Jesus had to rise from the dead.) Then the disciples went back to where they were staying.

Now Mary stood outside the tomb crying. As she wept, she bent over to look into the tomb and saw two angels in white, seated where Jesus' body had been, one at the head and the other at the foot.

They asked her, "Woman, why are you crying?"

"They have taken my Lord away," she said, "and I don't know where they have put him." 14 At this, she turned around and saw Jesus standing there, but she did not realize that it was Jesus.

He asked her, "Woman, why are you crying? Who is it you are looking for?"

Thinking he was the gardener, she said, "Sir, if you have carried him away, tell me where you have put him, and I will get him."

Jesus said to her, "Mary."

She turned toward him and cried out in Aramaic, "Rabboni!" (which means "Teacher").

Jesus said, "Do not hold on to me, for I have not yet ascended to the Father. Go instead to my brothers and tell them, 'I am ascending to my Father and your Father, to my God and your God.'"

Mary Magdalene went to the disciples with the news: "I have seen the Lord!" And she told them that he had said these things to her. (NIV)

Journal: Where have you "seen" the risen Jesus lately in your life?

What effect did it have on you?

How did you recognize that it was him?

How did it bring you to life inside?

Reflection:

easter

the silence was deafening
that early morning as she stood,
gripped by a love that would not release her
everyone else was gone
back to their homes and their families

"how could they forget so quickly?" she thought
as she stood in the first light of dawn,
tears streaming down her cheeks
"did they not feel it too . . . . the love?"
"if they did, how could they leave?"

her heart would not allow her to go
so she stayed — as near to him as she knew how
was she waiting?
was she hoping?
or was she simply doing the only thing she could —
to be near the place he was last near
she would rather be near him than anyone or anything
so she stayed . . . . and cried
longing to hear her name from his lips once more

and then suddenly the voice . . . . it startled her
looking through the tears she could not see who it was

"have you seen him?" she asked
"do you know where he is?"

it wasn't until he uttered her name
that she recognized his voice
and at its sweet sound

everything in her was raised to life again
it was easter you see . . . . and he had risen
and because of that
so had she

Pray: Pray that God would give you eyes to see the risen
Jesus in your life and world today.

Closing Prayer: Set me free, O Risen One, from all of my
misguided ways of being and seeing. Break the chains
that bind me and destroy my patterns of sin and
darkness and death. Set me free, Lord Jesus, and raise
me up to the new life you long for me to experience in
you. Amen.

Tuesday
First Week of Easter

Come to Stillness: Spend a few minutes in silence allowing your heart and soul to be still before God. Stillness will allow you to be awake and attentive to God and to recognize him in whatever way he might try to come to you today.

Opening Prayer: O Risen Jesus, help us to be open enough and attentive enough to recognize you when you come to walk alongside of us today. Amen.

Scripture: Luke 24:13-35

Now that same day two of them were going to a village called Emmaus, about seven miles from Jerusalem. They were talking with each other about everything that had happened. As they talked and discussed these things with each other, Jesus himself came up and walked along with them; but they were kept from recognizing him.

He asked them, "What are you discussing together as you walk along?"

They stood still, their faces downcast. One of them, named Cleopas, asked him, "Are you the only one visiting Jerusalem who does not know the things that have happened there in these days?"

"What things?" he asked.

"About Jesus of Nazareth," they replied. "He was a prophet, powerful in word and deed before God and all the people. The chief priests and our rulers handed him over to be sentenced to death, and they crucified him; but we had hoped that he was the one who was going to redeem Israel. And what is more, it is the third day since all this took place. In addition, some of our women amazed us. They went to the tomb early this morning but didn't find his body. They came and told us that they had seen a vision of angels, who said he was alive. Then some of our companions went to the tomb and found it just as the women had said, but they did not see Jesus."

He said to them, "How foolish you are, and how slow to believe all that the prophets have spoken! Did not the Messiah have to suffer these things and then enter his glory?" And beginning with Moses and all the Prophets, he explained to them what was said in all the Scriptures concerning himself.

As they approached the village to which they were going, Jesus continued on as if he were going farther. But they urged him strongly, "Stay with us, for it is nearly evening; the day is almost over." So he went in to stay with them.

When he was at the table with them, he took bread, gave thanks, broke it and began to give it to them. Then their eyes were opened and they recognized him, and he disappeared from their sight. They asked each other, "Were not our hearts burning within us while he talked with us on the road and opened the Scriptures to us?"

They got up and returned at once to Jerusalem. There they found the Eleven and those with them, assembled together and saying, "It is true! The Lord has risen and has appeared to Simon." Then the two told what had happened on the way, and how Jesus was recognized by them when he broke the bread. (NIV)

Journal: What about this story makes your heart burn within you? Why?

How have you recognized Jesus walking along with you lately?

What caused the Emmaus travelers to recognize Jesus?

What helps you recognize him?

Reflection:

emmaus

as you walk
pay attention
for i may come
and walk alongside you

for today
is the day
of resurrection
when all that is dead
within you
and around you
will be brought to life
once again

Pray: Pray that God would open your eyes to see the Risen Jesus this day.

Closing Prayer: Lord Jesus, help me to be attentive to your presence and your voice this day. Help me to not get so caught up in the comings and goings of it that I miss you completely. Thank you that you desire my company and my attention. Help me to give you both. Amen. (*Pieces II* by Jim Branch)

Wednesday
First Week of Easter

Come to Stillness: Spend a few minutes in silence allowing your heart and soul to be still before God. Rest in his presence. Allow the stillness to awaken you to his voice and his Spirit.

Opening Prayer: Lord Jesus, help me to cling not to the old patterns and old ways of being and seeing that I have become so used to and adept at, but help me to be made new each day, living a resurrected life, with your resurrection power. In the name of the resurrected One—Jesus. Amen.

Scripture: Luke 24:1-12

On the first day of the week, very early in the morning, the women took the spices they had prepared and went to the tomb. They found the stone rolled away from the tomb, but when they entered, they did not find the body of the Lord Jesus. While they were wondering about this, suddenly two men in clothes that gleamed like lightning stood beside them. In their fright the women bowed down with their faces to the ground, but the men said to them, "Why do you look for the living among the dead? He is not here; he has risen! Remember how he told you, while he was still with you in Galilee: 'The Son of Man must be delivered over to the hands of sinners, be crucified and on the third day be raised again.' " Then they remembered his words.

When they came back from the tomb, they told all these things to the Eleven and to all the others. It was Mary Magdalene, Joanna, Mary the mother of James, and the others with them who told this to the apostles. But they did not believe the women, because their words seemed to them like nonsense. Peter, however, got up and ran to the tomb. Bending over, he saw the strips of linen lying by themselves, and he went away, wondering to himself what had happened. (NIV)

Journal: Why do you look for the living among the dead?

Reflection:

alive

the view
from this side
of the stone
now rolled away
takes my breath
in awestruck wonder
who would've believed it

a new world received
spacious and free
fruitful and abundant
rich and full
alive

but o how difficult the terrain
and how long the journey
in arriving at this place
who could've imagined
in the midst of the pain
and the struggle
and the cross
that this new land
could be so beautiful

something had to die
in order for
something new
to be born

Pray: Ask God to show you the places in your life that need to die in order than something new and beautiful can be resurrected.

Closing Prayer: Teach me to seek you, for I cannot seek you unless you teach me, or find you unless you show yourself to me. Let me seek you in my desire, and desire you in my seeking. Let me find you by loving you, let me love you when I find you. ~St. Anselm

Thursday
First Week of Easter

Come to Stillness: Spend some time in silence allowing your heart and soul to come to rest. Just be fully present to God and to whatever he might want to do or say.

Opening Prayer: Lord Jesus, all too often I am filled with doubt. Come through the locked doors of my life and give me the ability to stop doubting and believe. Amen.

Scripture: John 20:19-28

On the evening of that first day of the week, when the disciples were together, with the doors locked for fear of the Jewish leaders, Jesus came and stood among them and said, "Peace be with you!" After he said this, he showed them his hands and side. The disciples were overjoyed when they saw the Lord.

Again Jesus said, "Peace be with you! As the Father has sent me, I am sending you." And with that he breathed on them and said, "Receive the Holy Spirit. If you forgive anyone's sins, their sins are forgiven; if you do not forgive them, they are not forgiven."

Now Thomas (also known as Didymus), one of the Twelve, was not with the disciples when Jesus came. So the other disciples told him, "We have seen the Lord!" But he said to them, "Unless I see the nail marks in his hands and put my finger where the nails were, and put my hand into his side, I will not believe."

A week later his disciples were in the house again, and Thomas was with them. Though the doors were locked, Jesus came and stood among them and said,

"Peace be with you!" Then he said to Thomas, "Put your finger here; see my hands. Reach out your hand and put it into my side. Stop doubting and believe."

Thomas said to him, "My Lord and my God!" (NIV)

Journal: Where is doubt living in you these days?

Who or what are you doubting?

How are you doubting God these days?

What will it take for you to believe?

Reflection: Okay, I have to admit it, I tend to give Thomas a bit of a hard time. Every time I read this story I'm like, "Come on man!" Thinking that maybe somehow I would not have had the same reaction. Who am I kidding? Maybe I have a hard time relating because my particular set of doubts doesn't look exactly like his. Which can lead me to believe (wrongly, I might add) that I don't struggle with doubt. Which is a complete joke. Of course I do! In fact, when I take any time at all to venture into this fragile heart of mine I quickly realize that I am filled with doubt. My doubt, however, does not tend to be the kind that makes me wonder if there is a God, or if he is really there. My doubt has more to do with really believing that God loves me and that I am of immense value to him. It seems that no matter how hard I try to convince myself, I just can't become fully persuaded that it's true. It's the old "it's not you, it's me" line. My doubt seems to have more to do with how I feel about myself than how I feel about my God. A wise saint once said that *the most important thing you believe about God is what you think God believes about you.* That's where the major breakdown is for me. And that sort of doubt has a significant impact on how I live my life.

Since I am filled with doubt about myself and my value it can make me pretty needy inside; constantly in search of affirmation, constantly in pursuit of achievement, constantly in need of acceptance, constantly seeking significance — all in order to somehow prove to myself and to my world that I am worth loving. Thus, I am often filled with insecurity and anxiety, especially when things are not going according to plan. That makes me frustrated, critical, and defensive; often causing me to see people more as threats and competitors than as human beings deserving my love and compassion.

And though I might not feel like my doubt is the same as that of Thomas, the words Jesus speaks to Thomas speak directly to me as well. *Jim, put your finger here; see my hands. Reach out your hand and put it into my side. This is how much I love you. Enough to allow all of this to be done to me. How can you possibly question my love? How can you possibly question your value? Stop doubting and believe!*

Which brings up the same reply (as that of Thomas) from deep within me: *"My Lord, and my God!"* I *believe.* And for a while all is well in my heart and life once again. That is, until I start to forget. That's why I have been trying to relive this encounter several times each day—whenever doubt or fear or insecurity or anxiety or frustration begin to rear their ugly head. And when I do, I hear my beloved Jesus once again telling me to *put your finger here, see my hands, and touch my side.* And once again his *truth has set me free.* Thanks be to God for his unfailing love and his relentless pursuit.

Pray: Talk with God about your places of doubt. Listen for his word in response.

Closing Prayer: My Lord and my God. Help me to believe in you, even when everything within me is filled with fear and doubt and questions. Come through my locked doors and show yourself to me in a way that drives out everything but belief and love. Amen.

Friday
First Week of Easter

Come to Stillness: Spend some time in silence allowing your heart and soul to come to rest. Just be fully present to God, aware of his presence, and attentive to his voice.

Opening Prayer: Lord Jesus, risen Savior, come to me, even though my doors might be locked in fear and doubt. Come to me and offer me your peace. Let me see your face. Let me hear your voice. Let me touch your wounds. And help me to believe. Amen.

Scripture: John 20:26-28

A week later his disciples were in the house again, and Thomas was with them. Though the doors were locked, Jesus came and stood among them and said, "Peace be with you!" Then he said to Thomas, "Put your finger here; see my hands. Reach out your hand and put it into my side. Stop doubting and believe."

Thomas said to him, "My Lord and my God!" (NIV)

Journal: Where is unbelief still living in you?

How does it show itself?

What will it take for you to truly believe?

Reflection:

Me: Lord, is my anxiety, at its core, really unbelief?
Jesus: *What do you think?*
Me: I'm afraid it is, but unbelief sounds like such an ugly, harsh word.
Jesus: *Unbelief has many faces. Unfortunately, anxiety is one of the faces you are most familiar with.*
Me: Well, that's really humbling. Because not a day goes by, and in some instances not a minute goes by, when I am not battling anxiety.
Jesus: *Then stop doubting and believe.*
Me: Is it really that easy?
Jesus: *I never said it was easy, but it is that simple. Most things in the spiritual life are.*
Me: How do I do that?
Jesus: *Look at what I did with Thomas, that will give you a hint. Jim, my deepest wish for you is my deepest wish for all of my sons and daughters – my peace. Which is not just a feeling, but the state of being whole and free. And you become whole and free by truly believing how deeply and passionately (and freely) you are loved.*
Me: I long to know that love and that peace more deeply, in a way that completely transforms everything about me.
Jesus: *Then put your finger here, touch my wounds. Reach out your hand and put it into my side. Stop doubting and believe. Stop doubting your value and your worth. Stop thinking that you must earn my love and affection. Stop trying so hard to prove to yourself and your world that you are worth loving. Stop doubting my love for you, instead touch my wounds and know that it's true. I love you. Believe it. Believe it with all your heart. Peace be with you!*
Me: My Lord and my God!

Pray: Place your areas of unbelief before God today and ask him to meet you in the middle of them. Ask him to reveal himself to you in a way that helps you to truly believe. Wait in silence as you watch and listen for his reply.

Closing Prayer: Lord, I believe, help my unbelief. Amen.

Saturday
First Week of Easter

Come to Stillness: Spend a few minutes in silence allowing your heart and soul to be still before God. Rest in his presence. Allow the stillness to awaken you to his voice and his Spirit.

Scripture: Matthew 28:1-10

When the Sabbath was over, just as the first day of the week was dawning Mary from Magdala and the other Mary went to look at the tomb. At that moment there was a great earthquake, for an angel of the Lord came down from Heaven, went forward and rolled back the stone and took his seat upon it. His appearance was dazzling like lightning and his clothes were white as snow. The guards shook with terror at the sight of him and collapsed like dead men. But the angel spoke to the women, "Do not be afraid. I know that you are looking for Jesus who was crucified. He is not here — he is risen, just as he said he would. Come and look at the place where he was lying. Then go quickly and tell his disciples that he has risen from the dead. And, listen, he goes before you into Galilee! You will see him there! Now I have told you my message."

Then the women went away quickly from the tomb, their hearts filled with awe and great joy, and ran to give the news to his disciples.

But quite suddenly, Jesus stood before them in their path, and said, "Peace be with you!" And they went forward to meet him and, clasping his feet, worshipped him. Then Jesus said to them, "Do not be afraid. Go now and tell my brothers to go into Galilee and they shall see me there." (JBP)

Journal: What stones need to be rolled away in your life?

What will it take?

Reflection:

> sometimes it takes an earthquake
> to roll the stone away
> God sends his angel
> to disrupt or disturb
> to shake or quake
> our lives and our world
> just enough so that
> the stone that held us captive
> a prisoner trapped in the dark gloom
> of death and despair
> is rolled away
> from the tomb
> and we are given
> the power
> and freedom and possibility
> of leaving the stench
> and decay of death behind
> and stepping out into the warmth
> and light of new life
> alive. risen. resurrected.
> O God, let us take that step

Pray: Ask God to show you where you are still living as if the stone has not been rolled away.

Closing Prayer: Lord Jesus, roll the stones away from the tombs in my life, even if it takes an earthquake. Amen.

A Final Thought

What does resurrection look like for us, this side of heaven? What should we expect? What should we hope for? And how should we expect it to unfold? My guess is that if we've learned anything at all these last few weeks from the stories of the resurrection in Scripture, it is to expect the unexpected. But I keep wondering, what does resurrection look like in our present lives? Does it come suddenly? Like the earthquake that shook the tomb and rolled the stone away in Matthew? Or does it come in a more hidden way, as it did to the travelers on the road to Emmaus; so slowly and subtly that we will have to pay careful attention to be able to recognize it? Or will it be a long, slow process; like a journey in which the destination appears on the horizon, off in the distance, but still seems miles and miles away from a current reality? You know that it is getting closer, slowly but surely, but can't quite tell exactly when it will arrive.

I guess I'm wondering because of my hope that at some point this old, passing, manufactured, false self will finally be fully put to death and the new, eternal, God-breathed, true self will rise from the ashes. But for now I still have way more of one than I'd like, and less of the other than I truly long for. The old just keeps hanging around, with nowhere near the amount of life it once had mind you, but ever-present nonetheless. And the new, although it keeps gaining more of a presence and a voice within me, still is not in complete control of my thinking and my believing, my being and my doing. How much longer will this wrestling go on before I wrestle no more and am able to rest in the fullness of all that I was created to be?

I suppose that my part in this journey is to trust that somehow God is in control of it all. It is his work and not my own. My part is to continually take that next step toward him, whatever that may look like and wherever that may lead. For, when I focus on the big picture, I can easily get overwhelmed and discouraged at the distance that must be covered. But when I simply focus on taking that next step, and trusting him with the rest, it somehow feels more hopeful. And isn't that what this season is all about?

Peace be with you!

Jim

Closing Prayer: Thank you, O God, that spring always follows winter, that Easter always follows Good Friday, and that resurrection always follows death!!! We are so grateful that death does not have the final word — life does. We praise you, O God of life! Amen!

by his wounds

not my hands, my hands
not my feet, my feet
not my friends, my friends
but my god, my god*

this shows the true agony
of that horrific moment
when you lord jesus
cried out in the dark

it was not the physical pain
that finally made you scream
it wasn't the flogging
or the thorns
or even the nails

nor was it the emotional pain
that caused you to groan
it wasn't the denial
or the betrayal
or even the abandonment of friends

it was the spiritual pain
that finally broke your heart
for all of the sin
and all of the pain
and all of the suffering
of all of the world
was placed upon you
and for the very first time
you were separated completely
from divine love

and god himself mourned
the loss of his beloved son
and tore his heavenly robes
in grief and sadness
as the curtain of the temple
was torn in two
from top to bottom

the sun hid its face
the earth shook its head
and trembled at the sight
the rocks split in half
the tombs gave up their dead
and the centurion looked on
in amazement

for lord jesus
your cry from the cross
is also the cry of our hearts
in our darkest moments
we too scream out
my god, my god
why have you forsaken me

so from the cross
you not only said,
"i get it"
i know the depths
of your sorrow
but you also said,
"i'll take it"
i'll take all of your sin
and all of your pain
and all of your suffering

and all of your brokenness
as well as that of all people
from all ages
on myself

for by my wounds
you are healed

inspired by the sermons of Timothy Keller

Made in the USA
Las Vegas, NV
24 February 2022